£ 2·00

Foreword by George Carey
former Archbishop of Canterbury

The ONE BIG QUESTION
THE GOD OF LOVE IN A WORLD OF SUFFERING

CWR

Contents

Acknowledgements

My biggest gratitude is to my wife, Myrtle: for her deep faith and love, the example of her life, her personal handling of suffering, her strong encouragement to me to write this book, and her patient support throughout the whole process, as well as for being a very perceptive reader of the script. My thanks, too, to our family for their loving support – Graham and Rachel, Phil and Liz, Andrew and Rachel – in this, and always.

My thanks next to CWR who asked to publish this book, and to the whole CWR team, especially Lynette Brooks (Director of Publishing), Sue Wavre (Senior Editor), Sheila Jacobs (editing), June Bradley (copyrights). Everyone has acted with gracious professionalism and warm Christian encouragement

I hesitated to ask Archbishop George Carey whether he would write a foreword but, when I did, he responded with alacrity and enthusiasm. The foreword he has written is masterly, with its theological depth and its compassionate understanding, all arising from first-hand experience across the world, and in his own family. I am most grateful to him.

Fiona Castle is an inspiring speaker and witness for Christ and has shown how the sad death of her fine husband Roy from cancer has not soured her faith but rather deepened it. I was touched by her kindness in agreeing to read the book and much appreciate her warm and thoughtful commendation.

So many others have generously and kindly allowed me to quote from their writings or speaking, and several have written specially for this book from their suffering, particularly Bob Mortimer, Mel Menzies, the Very Revd John Benson and the Revd Sharon Grenham-Toze. Conversations with the Revd Dr John Stott have been much appreciated. The Revd Michael Wenham, Abigail Witchalls, Celia Harding and Ruth Caiger have most kindly responded. I have expressed my thanks to them in the notes at the end of each chapter. I have been touched that scientists as well as theologians have taken trouble to correspond, to advise on and to check material. Dr Colin Connolly went more than the extra mile for me, and I am much in his debt. Michael Buerk also kindly corresponded with me.

I appreciated the offer from Leslie Roberts to edit the first draft of the manuscript, and he took much care on it; Frances MacKenney-Jeffs also helped considerably from her own research by supplying information on a wide variety of books on this theme, and in sharing her own pilgrimage; Judge David Turner, QC and Judge Diana Faber gave thoughtful reflections on justice (but I alone am responsible for what I have written!); Dr Ian Cunliffe advised medically; Elizabeth Baughen advised on counselling; Sheila Lonsdale paid close attention to the reading of the manuscript, and gave many comments; Margaret Mortimer generously allowed me to include Bob's contributions to the book, even though his earthly life ended last year; she also read the manuscript, as did Graham Sopp, Rachel Baughen and Sandra Pronger. I am most grateful to them all. My thanks, too, to the congregations of St James, Clerkenwell and St Saviours, Guildford who received a series of sermons from me on this theme and responded helpfully with comments and questions, as well as sharing personal experiences of suffering.

The example of so many who have turned personal suffering into a 'theatre of grace' has been much of a stimulus for this book – but, most of all, it sprang from the desire that all who have faith in Christ will more fully be able to join with Paul and say from the heart: 'Praise be to the God and Father of our Lord Jesus Christ, the Father of compassion and the God of all comfort, who comforts us in all our troubles' (2 Cor. 1:3–4).

Michael Baughen, June 2010.

Foreword

There can be little doubt that the problem of pain with the bundle of issues that accompany it forms the most grievous obstacle to believing in God. Following the First World War, Raymond Asquith, son of the then prime minister, wrote bitterly, 'A blind God stomps around the globe with a pair of sensitively malevolent antennae seeking what deserves to live and using iron hooves to grind it to dust'. So it might seem at times.

It therefore takes a very bold writer to tackle this problem head-on with intelligence, compassion and without minimising the extent of the difficulties for Christian belief. Bishop Michael Baughen brings to this task his rich experience as a Christian minister, and his years of thinking around this most contentious of subjects. He deals with the subject with sensitivity and much understanding. He brings out the fact that if the problem of pain and inexplicable suffering challenges the person of faith, so does the problem of good for those who reject, out of hand, the idea of a good God. If purposelessness and randomness reign in our universe, where do goodness, justice, sacrifice come from? Why is it that in spite of the most terrible things happening to people of faith, they refuse to believe in futility?

Perhaps one of the most terrible incidents that came the way of my wife and I was in early 1995 when we were among the very first Westerners to visit Rwanda. We flew to a Roman Catholic cathedral some miles from Kigali where 5,000 women and children had been murdered. The bones of the people were still there, in and around the cathedral. Our eyes stung with tears as we imagined the people pleading for mercy, in vain. But the people we met refused to conclude that a blind God deliberately allowed this terrible act to happen. Rather, they insisted that man's sin and evil was the originating cause. From that awful event so many good things have emerged with people on both sides of the conflict determined to create a new society.

However, we must be frank, as Michael Baughen is, that there is no one simple answer that can satisfy the mind searching for answers to what theologians call divine justice (theodicy). That surely should not surprise us because if God is anything, He is greater than our minds can comprehend or even imagine. The heart of Christian teaching is, however, that we can know Him through Jesus Christ and we may grasp His purposes through intelligent faith.

As the writer shows, Christians are not left to live as orphans with questions only. A real faith opens the door to a new and exciting relationship with Christ: a relationship that gives strength and courage to face each day with hope and wonder. This book encourages Christians who are living with suffering to know more of God's strength even in weakness. I am glad it is full of stories of Christians who have faced pain and death with courage and faith, because that is the living reality of what faith actually means. Years ago I recall visiting a parishioner in Durham who was dying of cancer. I must have looked very miserable because the lady looked up at me and said with a big smile on her face: 'Why are you looking so miserable, vicar. I'm only dying, you know!' Some thirty years on I still remember those words as though they were minted yesterday. 'I'm only dying, you know' is a statement by a Christian who knows that this life, though it must not be scorned, is but the gateway to a glorious kingdom that God has prepared for those who love Him.

We are in Bishop Michael Baughen's debt with this powerful and stimulating book. Unafraid, he faces head-on this most intractable of problems without falling into glibness or facile explanations. The truth is that we cannot adequately explain suffering and evil. There is only one possible answer to the question: 'Why does God allow such evil?' and it lies in the fact that God Himself is involved in the pain, the suffering and the evil and the ultimate heart of it is the cross of Christ. Only with God's total identification with human suffering can the moral accusation be removed. And what a wonderful destiny that gives to all of us who follow that cross.

George Carey
Archbishop of Canterbury, 1991–2002

Why? How? An introduction

Why? Why? Why?

'Why?' is a question that never seems to go away with respect to suffering:

> *'Why has this happened to me?'*
> *'Why does a God of love allow suffering?'*
> *'Why is it that the evildoers seem to succeed and the good do not? I thought God was a God of justice.'*
> *'Why does God allow natural disasters like tsunamis?'*
> *'Why doesn't God stop earthquakes?'*
> *'Why doesn't God stop all the wars and conflicts in the world?'*
> *'Why does God allow so many Christians to be persecuted, evicted from their homes and even murdered because of their faith?'*

As I stood on an Underground platform waiting for my train, I noticed a girl jigging to the music coming through her earphones. Her mother was asking her a question. The jigging went on. The mother raised her voice. The jigging went on. It was only when the mother shouted loudly and the crowd on the platform moved forward to join in the shouting that the girl became aware of what was happening and took off her earphones. *Only when the block was removed could she hear anything other than her own music.*

The biggest block against facing up to 'real' Christianity is suffering. It is like those earphones. Gospel truth may be explained, emphasised and made as clear as possible, but, if there is a block caused by the issue of God and suffering, there is unlikely to be any response. For many people, the block is like steel shutters that form an almost impenetrable barrier to faith.

This block is so often hidden by a smokescreen of intellectual argument. I think of a person who had held a high position. When we first met, his arguments against Christianity were all intellectual.

Professor Dawkins was a star and his views were accepted without question. Then, when that star faded, the argument was changed from atheism to agnosticism, largely based on John Humphrys' tenets in his book In God We Doubt.[1] The Darwinian celebration came next, and evolution became the ground of discussion. Yet, even then, I was able to draw on brilliant books by Christians in that field which convinced him it was still possible to believe in God. Eventually, however, the debate stalled. I discovered that the real block was the issue of suffering, and sadly all discussion on this was refused as being 'too hurtful a memory to discuss'. Emotional involvement in suffering had overwhelmed intellect.

Charles Darwin did not, apparently, lose his faith in God because of his theories, but mainly because of his personal sufferings, in particular the death of his young daughter.

C.S. Lewis, who had previously been able to think through the problem of pain so thoroughly and brilliantly, became so overwhelmed by emotion at the death of his wife that he only slowly found his way out of it, as he so powerfully described in A Grief Observed.[2]

And when a fine Christian leader and good friend of mine lost his young wife, he commented, bitterly, 'Prayer is a lottery.'

Even for those with the deepest faith, sadness and the sense of loss can flood the soul and bring a sense of God-forsakenness.

Sadly, some Christians, who think they know all the answers when it comes to suffering, quickly turn their backs on God when tragedy strikes them personally, crying out angrily 'But it wasn't supposed to happen to me!'

For some people, it is not so much personal suffering, but the vast amounts of suffering in the world at large, such as poverty, hunger, persecution and homelessness, which put their faith in a Sovereign Deity in doubt.

Young people, for example, are often deeply moved when on their gap years they encounter extreme pain and suffering in war-torn or famine-ravaged parts of Africa and Asia, and find the contrast with their own privileged upbringings almost too much to bear. Their comfortable faith in God is challenged, even shattered.

Visitors to Holocaust sites, seeing the stark evidence of the horrendous inequalities and evil in the world, raise poignant questions about justice and mercy, about God and suffering.

In the affluent West, many Christians would say they have a comfortable life most of the time. Their faith is well-nurtured. They experience fellowship with one another. They believe that, as long as they pray regularly and take an active part in the life of their local church, everything will be all right. But then comes the unexpected ... plans for a wedding are shattered by the unfaithfulness of the person they were going to marry; their 'safe' job becomes redundant overnight; a loved one is struck down with a debilitating illness. Until this point, the question of suffering has only been considered occasionally. No thought-through convictions have been established. It has been too easy to take Romans 8:28 out of context and assume that all things will work together for their personal good if they love God, and that life will be a 'bed of roses'.

The aim of Section A in this book is to try to tackle a number of the questions thrown at Christians about suffering. The hope is that those turned off from God will read and at least consider the responses that are suggested (there will only be full answers in heaven). It is also hoped that believers in the Lord Jesus Christ can become better equipped not only to deal with their own tragedies, but to be able to give informed responses when genuine seekers, whether agnostics and atheists, ask them 'But why?'

When a block in a water pipe is removed, the flow of water starts with a sudden and powerful force. This is often the case when the 'suffering block' is exposed and moved. There often comes an immediate receptivity to Scripture and the gospel. But first, the block has to be removed!

How? How? How?

The Bible supplies no thorough solution to the problem of evil, whether 'natural' evil or 'moral', that is, whether in the form of suffering or of sin. Its purpose is more practical than philosophical. Consequently, although there are references to sin and suffering on virtually every page, its concern is not to explain their origin but to help us to overcome them. (John Stott)[3]

So Christians need to know how to prepare for, and handle, suffering.

When we go to a hotel, there are escape procedures detailed on the bedroom door, and we are advised to see where the escape doors are situated; when we board an aircraft, we are always told the safety procedures, the positions of escape doors, how to handle emergency oxygen supply and how to put on and tie a life jacket. If we listen (do we?), we will be prepared should need arise.

In a similar way, we need to prepare ourselves to face any sufferings, trauma or turmoil that may come in our lives so that we do not collapse if and when they come. The way to prepare is to get our roots down deep into the great teachings of the Bible about suffering. We cannot know the detail of the suffering we may have to endure, but we can establish our principles of response and action. If we have prayerfully thought things through beforehand, then we will be in a much better position to cope.

In particular we need, all through life, to go on strengthening the three main pillars of the Christian life. They are the pillars of faith, love and hope and, of course, they stand on the rock of Christ. Almost everything else is built around them, and they are the pillars that need to withstand anything thrown at them. We look at each of these pillars and at building them more strongly in Chapters 9, 10 and 11.

The New Testament is full of passages on positive faith, on endurance, and on turning suffering into a way of glorifying our Lord. Suffering is seen as a means of spiritual growth and a sphere of powerful witness. It can be liberating, uplifting and challenging, and it can transform our thinking, our living … and our suffering! For me, the discovery of this in the vibrant writings of Paul and other apostles was a transforming experience, and Paul's passion for it is infectious! Yet, when Paul writes in Romans 8:18, 'I consider that our present sufferings are not worth comparing with the glory that will be revealed in us' his use of the Greek word translated as 'consider' indicates that his is a position that has only been arrived at after much thinking, praying, soul-searching and meditation. It is a position forged in strength through persecution, imprisonment, exhausting mission journeys and personal illness. It is tested and proven. It is an unshakeable conviction – and, by God's grace, this is the position to which we all need to come.

Some close Christian friends recently had to handle the shattering news of the husband's inoperable cancer. They rocked humanly (there is no need for a 'stiff upper lip' as a Christian – we *can* cry), but they did not rock spiritually. Although the treatment he received was the best, gradually the physical battle was lost. The pain, the disfigurement and the suffering were intense, but faith held. He died in the arms of Christ. I acted as 'devil's advocate' to his widow as I said, 'How can you possibly still believe in a God of love when you have seen such suffering in your beloved husband, and endured it yourself in walking this awful path with him?' She looked at me with amazement: 'Are you serious? Abandon faith in the God who has carried us, who has been so wonderfully with us through these months, whose love has surrounded us? How could I?' Because they had thought through the question of suffering *before* it had occurred, they had forged their convictions and faith more deeply in the heat of that suffering. Yes, there were tears. Yes, there was pain. But there was faith and great glory to God.

The issue of suffering, of course, is inextricably linked with the important arena of healing. There are many books on healing but few on suffering, yet everyone in the world experiences suffering and it is there on page after page of the Scriptures, from honest despair and a sense of devastation in the Psalms and the Prophets, to glorying in it for Christ in the New Testament. That is what we will look at in the second section of the book.

The last three chapters of this book look at the place of prayer in suffering and for healing. To concentrate on healing and to teach or imply that suffering is unnecessary for a Christian or is due to a lack of faith, or is because of some hidden sin, is to leave a trail of destruction. The Bible teaches *both* about handling suffering to God's glory *and* about the approach to healing for His glory. We need to have a theology of *both* and must keep them in balance to avoid over-despair on the one hand, or overconfidence on the other.

Our suffering in the West needs to be put in context. It is for many a very deep valley to go through, but the suffering endured by millions in the areas of the world devastated by conflict, famine and poverty is in a different dimension. These people are very much our 'neighbours' in this world, and Christian churches are strongly involved in helping the poor and suffering.

We also have a special concern for our Christian brothers and sisters in those parts of the world where they find themselves in the minority, and where new converts are regularly imprisoned without trial, stripped, beaten and even murdered. They may be forced out of their homes because of death threats (as happened to 12,000 souls in Mosul, Iraq). Their homes and churches may be burnt down (as happened in Nigeria). They may be burnt to death while taking refuge inside church (as occurred in India). It is vital that we seek to stand with them and to help them, as far as possible, with practical and spiritual support.

Archbishop Benkwashi of Nigeria, speaking at a Christian gathering in the UK in 2009, told his audience not to fear suffering. Despite having his house burnt down, his church burnt down, and being subjected to death threats and to violent attacks on both himself and his wife, he was able to say that *all* his suffering had *strengthened* both his faith and evangelistic resolve.

A text like 1 Peter 5:9–10 snaps into focus: 'standing firm in the faith, because you know that your brothers throughout the world are undergoing the same kind of sufferings. And the God of all grace, who called you to his eternal glory in Christ, after you have suffered a little while, will himself restore you and make you strong, firm and steadfast.'

NOTES
1   John Humphrys, *In God We Doubt* (London: Hodder & Stoughton, 2007).
2   C.S. Lewis, *A Grief Observed*, copyright © C.S. Lewis Pte. Limited, 1961.
    Extract reprinted by permission.
3   John R.W. Stott, *The Cross of Christ* (Leicester: IVP, 1986), p.312.
    My thanks to John for allowing me to quote him freely.

SECTION A
WHY?
QUESTIONING THE GOD OF LOVE

ONE

Why is there suffering if there is a God of love?

In the hospital ward the atmosphere was highly charged. A precious child had just died of meningitis. She had always been a healthy youngster, but then came the fever, the stiff neck, the vomiting. The diagnosis and treatment had been too late. Although the family didn't go to church other than at Easter and Christmas, they had always regarded themselves as Christians. And they could still remember enough of the Bible to know that it speaks of God as love. In their grief, the heart-cry of accusation came rapidly: *'How could a God of love allow our child to die?'*

The question is voiced time and time again – when a loved one dies of cancer, one's marriage partner, with Alzheimer's, slides away from recognising us, an eighteen-year-old has a head-on road crash, a son is killed by a terrorist bullet while serving in the armed forces, a friend drops dead with a heart attack, or we ourselves experience physical suffering, or read about it in other parts of the world. It is a natural enough question. It springs from agonised hearts. It is often followed up with, 'if I loved someone and had the power to stop their suffering or to meet their need, I would do it. So if God is all-powerful, as well as being love, then why doesn't He do the same?'

This accusation against God for allowing, not stopping, suffering will be taken up in subsequent chapters but, in this chapter, we look at what is actually meant by 'a God of love'.

When I was a boy, there was a catchphrase that emanated from a popular philosopher called C.E.M. Joad[1]: 'It depends what you mean by [such and such].' We need to say the same now. We need to ask, 'What do we mean by love, and by a God of love?'

For some people, this is an attractive phrase they picked up in a school assembly or some other brief encounter with Christianity. God is looked on as a divine grandfather with a kind face and a pocketful of goodies, who is there to sort everything out for us, who does His best to intervene when we are in trouble, and who will do what we ask.

Others feel that God is there to be used, to get what they can out of Him, and to be dispensed with when He doesn't deliver. Some may even attend church 'religiously' every week, but they see it merely as an insurance policy to keep on the right side of His divine wrath. Others disregard Him, make fun of Him, or have some vague, distant notion of a 'higher power' or 'mysterious cosmic entity'. God is treated like one of the Emergency Services ... called on immediately when there is a problem, but happily ignored at all other times. When people say they have lost their faith in God, I tell them I am delighted because the quicker they get rid of their false idea of a god, the quicker they can begin to find the true God.

Ironically, while they expect God to respond because He is a 'God of love', there is no thought of returning that love. Yet this would be an amazing presumption in human relationships, and we are talking here of Almighty God!

All these pictures of God have little to do with what the Bible says about getting close to Him, learning about Him, knowing Him personally, and being in a relationship of love and worship with Him.

The breakdown of a love relationship can cause immense pain. For instance, we may have a renegade son who throws back in our face all the love, kindness and provision we have showered on him as he grows up. He rejects us, our values, our way of life ... but most of all, he rejects our love. Though we may be able to go on loving him, we may need to refuse to do anything he wants, or to give him anything he wants, because he is just using us and does not love us. The relationship is broken and abused.

The same breakdown in relationship can happen between us and God. The story of the prodigal son (Luke 15:11–32) shows us God's attitude when we become renegade sons and daughters. The son takes his inheritance and turns his back on the father but, even though his riotous living eventually leaves him friendless and in poverty, the father does not intervene. While the father never ceases to love him, he knows that if he sends his son more money, it will only be misused and this will achieve nothing. The experience of deprivation and suffering (for which the father was, of course, not responsible) actually brings the son to his senses, and he sees where true love and value lie. This was not the purpose of his suffering, but it helped him face up to life and its values (as it often does, even when the suffering is not our fault) and, especially, it made him turn back to the father. When the son turns back with repentance in his heart, the father runs to meet him (the only time in the Bible that God is in a hurry!).

As an anonymous person once said: 'Suffering is not a question that demands an answer; it is not a problem that demands a solution; it is a mystery which demands a presence.'

From the very beginning, God's intention has been to be in a relationship with us. Genesis 2–3 records how this was thrown away by our rebellion. Yet God did not give up on us. Ever since, He has persisted and has gone to extremes to make it possible for us to be forgiven and restored into a relationship with Him – 'God demonstrates his own love for us in this: While we were still sinners, Christ died for us' (Rom. 5:8).

*　　*　　*　　*　　*

So, when we come into a living relationship with the Lord Jesus Christ, does that mean that everything changes for us, including suffering? The answer is both 'No' and 'Yes'!

'No', because suffering is part of the fallen world in which we live, and we are all affected by it and by sin, by the use and abuse of free will, by injustice, wars, illnesses and physical mortality. D.A. Carson describes suffering as 'the effluent of the fall'.[2] Those who are restored into a living relationship with God do not get removed from this fallen world until death, like every other human being, and we are not meanwhile placed in some divine cocoon protecting us from all diseases and accidents. We share, like everyone else, in what Paul calls this 'groaning creation' (see Rom. 8:22). Although we have the first fruits of the Spirit, we 'groan inwardly as we wait eagerly for our adoption as sons, the redemption of our bodies' (Rom. 8:23). That will be in a new heaven and new earth where pain and suffering are no more.

'Yes', because although we share life and its sufferings like anyone else, we do so with God's steadfast love surrounding us. That is the *huge* difference. Everything is transformed by that love – our faith, our attitude to suffering, and our handling of it for God's glory. Most of all it means that, whatever we face, God is with us. This is what the 'love of God' means to us in the voyage of life, whether in calm or rough seas, and *especially* in the rough seas of suffering.

When Mike Harding, priest,[3] was dying of cancer, he described this relationship as a 'presence':

> like sitting in front of an open log fire on a cold and blustery winter's day. And simply enjoying the comfort and security that the experience provides. The only difference being that in this case the comfort and security is constant. The fire never goes out and never has to be re-made. This relationship, therefore, takes on such intensity that it allows no possibility of separation save that which may be chosen by the individual himself from moment to moment. The actual process of dying – the gradual loss of bodily functions and faculties – even the 'last enemy' death itself, cannot thus diminish this relationship by a single degree.

Psalm 23 shows superbly that, although we may know the Lord as our shepherd in the green pastures and still waters, our relationship with Him deepens in the testing of the valley of the shadow. The psalmist begins to speak of the Lord in very personal terms – 'you are with me' (italics mine). The valley is not removed, but he finds God holding him, encouraging him, comforting him ('your rod and your staff ... comfort me' in verse 4); he finds that he no longer fears evil (v.4); he receives special touches of love – a prepared table, an anointing with oil, even when he is surrounded by his enemies (v.5). The climax of the psalm shows him realising the depth of God's goodness and love that surround him for the whole of life and beyond. Paul expresses the same truth powerfully in Romans 8:35–37: 'Who shall separate us from the love of Christ? Shall trouble or hardship or persecution or famine or nakedness or danger or sword? … No, in all these things we are more than conquerors through him who loved us.'

Bob Mortimer was a fit and healthy man who climbed mountains and loved to undertake rugged walks and adventures. He was a probation officer before retirement. He was a fine Christian. When his cancer was diagnosed, I asked him to write down his experiences, and he and his wife, Margaret, most kindly agreed that they could be printed. Extracts of his story appear throughout the book. This is the first one:

In February 2006 I was diagnosed with cancer. It came right out of the blue – I had always prided myself on my health and fitness (I think pride was probably the right word for it!), and I was quite unprepared for the prospect of serious illness. I went through the whole gamut of feelings and emotions; disbelief ('surely this could not happen to me'), fear and panic. Then came the admission to hospital and surgery, followed by another blow – the cancer was aggressive and the prognosis poor. A subsequent course of radiotherapy left me with feelings of physical and emotional weakness of a kind I had never experienced before – and I felt generally at a low ebb. Nevertheless, as the weeks passed I began to feel stronger, so it was all the more disappointing to learn, following further scans in October 2007, that the cancer had returned.

People sometimes ask me how I have coped with this roller-coaster journey and I think it is important to emphasise that what follows is not a testimony to what I have achieved, but to the faithfulness of God and what I believe He has been trying to teach me through these experiences. There have been plenty of times when my faith has faltered, when I have become overwhelmed with the depressing nature of my immediate circumstances and have failed to draw on the resources of strength and grace available through Him. But the Lord has always been there for me and, not infrequently, at the low points of the journey, something *has occurred to lift my spirits – perhaps a particularly helpful card or visit from a praying friend, or the impact of a moving hymn or song – and I have been enabled, once again, to recognise and experience 'His strength made perfect in weakness.' I think it is true to say therefore, that through all the ups and downs of the past two years, both Margaret and I have known a remarkable sense of the presence and peace of God.*

*   *   *   *   *

Only through the Scriptures can we understand God as love. We will not find this anywhere else. It was C.S. Lewis who said that, when he was an atheist, it had never occurred to him to ask the question, 'If the universe is so bad, or even half so bad, how on earth did human beings ever come to attribute it to a wise and good Creator?'[4] Similarly, we would ask, 'How, in a world of so much evil, can humans have come to believe in a God of love?' Indeed, when humans create their own religions they are often prompted by fear. We see it in primitive offerings to placate imaginary gods who might otherwise hurt us, destroy us, or stop the fertility of the ground. So many of these 'gods' are terrifying. Religions can also put the stress on obeying laws and performing religious duties, where love is earned but does not exist as a relationship.

In 1966, Bilquis Sheikh, a high-born Pakistani woman and a Muslim, came to a living faith in Christ (for which she was ostracised and threatened with death). When she wrote a book about this, she entitled it I Dared to Call Him Father.[5] It was daring because she had been brought up to see God as a great God who must be worshipped and obeyed, but without any idea that a personal relationship with Him could exist. Christians can often take the Fatherhood of God for granted, as most of us learn to pray, 'Our Father ...' from an early age. Yet, for Bilquis Sheikh, it was thrilling, amazing and overwhelmingly wonderful to know God in personal relationship as her Father.

This relationship is only possible through Christ. We only learn this through the Scriptures, but it is not just a truth in our minds; it is also shown to us when we turn to Christ and experience this new relationship through the Holy Spirit in our hearts and lives –

> *those who are led by the Spirit of God are sons of God. For you did not receive a spirit that makes you a slave again to fear, but you received the Spirit of sonship. And by him we cry, "Abba, Father." The Spirit himself testifies with our spirit that we are God's children. Now if we are children, then we are heirs – heirs of God and co-heirs with Christ, if indeed we share in his sufferings in order that we may also share in his glory'* (Rom. 8:14–17).

This passage immediately precedes, and thus prepares us for, the rest of Romans 8, which confronts suffering.

It is in this love-relationship, as sons and daughters of our heavenly Father, that the Christian believer is held through all the experiences of life. Even when we do not understand the 'why?' we can put ourselves into the arms of God's love.

A text that has meant so much to me, and which I have commended to many people in their suffering, from Psalm 63:8, is 'My soul clings to you' or, in other translations, 'I cling to you' (GNB). The context is suffering. Earlier in the psalm, the psalmist had spoken of his hunger for God, his belief that God's love is better than life, and he had prayed. By this stage, however, he is only holding on by his fingertips. But then comes the line 'your right hand upholds me' (v.8). A faith that holds on is our part. The upholding hand is God's part. Here is love, unfailing love. God, in His love, is always upholding us. Countless believers through the centuries have testified to experiencing the truth of this in their suffering. It is this that transforms everything for the believer; it is this that confounds the unbeliever.

To conclude this chapter, I want to emphasise that, in considering love and suffering, we have to bring ourselves back to the cross of Christ. Suffering is at the centre of God's love. It is on the cross that we see God taking on Himself the evil and sin of humanity, with its pain and suffering and cruelty. Down the centuries, holy people have seen the sufferings of our Lord on the cross as an example to us in our own sufferings. Frances Young, the Methodist minister, writes in her moving book about bringing up her severely handicapped child, 'There could not be any philosophical answer to the problem of evil; not one is fully satisfactory. The only answer, the only thing that makes it possible to believe in God at all, is the cross.'[6] Similarly, John Stott, writing on suffering in his great book *The Cross of Christ*[7] says, 'I could never believe in God if it were not for the cross.'

We join in everlasting praise that we do not have a God who is detached, but One who has lived as a human and suffered. It was, says John 3:16, God's love for the world that caused Him to send His only begotten Son into the world. The cost of that love, culminating in the cross, was huge. Isaiah 53:3, and the following verses, describes it starkly: 'He was despised and rejected by men, a man of sorrows, and familiar with suffering ... afflicted ... pierced ... crushed ... wounds ... oppressed ... led like a lamb to the slaughter' (see Isa. 53:1–7). As 1 John 4:10 puts it, 'This is love: not that we loved God, but that he loved us and sent his Son as an atoning sacrifice for our sins.'

NOTES
1   Professor C.E.M. Joad (1891–1953) was an English philosopher and broadcasting personality. He popularised philosophy. He became famous through *The Brains Trust* on the radio, with Commander A.B. Campbell and Julian Huxley.
2   D.A. Carson, *How Long, O Lord?* (Leicester: IVP, 1982), p.48.
3   Mike Harding. See notes for Chapter 11.
4   C.S. Lewis, *The Problem of Pain*, copyright © C.S. Lewis Pte. Limited, 1941. Extract reprinted by permission.
5   Bilquis Sheikh with Richard Schneider, *I Dared to Call Him Father* (Eastbourne: Kingsway Publications, 1979).
6   Frances Young, *Face to Face* (London: Epworth Press, 1985), p.58.
7   John Stott, *The Cross of Christ* (Leicester: IVP, 1986), p.335. My thanks to him.

TWO

Why doesn't God stop all suffering, if He is omnipotent?

'If I Ruled the World' ... the original song with that title spoke in terms of happiness for everyone and the recent rap version wants everyone to have designer clothes! It has a terrific tune and the words echo human longing, but imagine hearing it in the midst of a bombing raid, when being made a refugee, when living in fear, when being told you will be paraplegic for life, or you are given the news that you have a terminal illness. The reaction might well be, 'If there is an all-powerful God, why can't He be like that, instead of letting us go through what we are going through?'

Humans have always sensed there must be something better than the frustrations of life on earth, even though there is also so much to enjoy and benefit from in the world. William Hazlitt said that 'man is the only animal that laughs and weeps, for he is the only animal that is struck with the difference between what things are and what they ought to be.'[1]

The Bible view is that this longing is because of 'The true light that gives light to everyone' (John 1:9, TNIV), that is, the light of the Son of God. Similarly, Ecclesiastes 3:11 says that God has 'set eternity in the human heart' (TNIV). We are restless until we find our rest in God. For the believer, who has the foretaste of the Spirit and of heaven, what is longed for becomes specific, and the longing becomes stronger!

The problem some of us create for ourselves is that we want heaven now. We're not interested in the tension between the 'now' and the 'not yet'. We say we want a world in which God stops all suffering and evil. If humans behaved as automatons, this would be perfectly possible. We could be programmed only to be kind. We could be programmed always to do God's will. We could be programmed to be satisfied with our puppet-like status, for we would know no other. It would be like a totalitarian state that is cut off from outside news and contact, where everyone is controlled and brainwashed to think what the controlling power requires them to think. This is what happened in Albania, where the regime tried to convince the people that they were leading the world, that others admired them for getting rid of religion, and that they were living in the best nation on earth. But many people in Albania longed for freedom from that crushing atheist regime and risked their lives trying to get across the straits to Corfu, defying the gun-posts all along the coast.

The film The Truman Show was about a young man who was brought up in a totally false world. His world was, in fact, a giant television studio and everyone in it was an actor except Truman. It was a 'perfect' world because it was entirely under the direction of the producer. Truman's daily life was watched by millions in 24-hour TV broadcasting. Eventually, however, he got restless and wanted freedom, going to desperate lengths to obtain it. The viewers in the real world cheered him on until he broke out. They wanted him to have freedom too.

The world that many think we should live in could only be like that if it was entirely controlled, a kind of divine Truman Show. We would be deeply frustrated because free will is built into us by our Creator, or, as Archbishop Rowan Williams said, 'we all want to be in charge'.[2]

Similarly, love cannot be forced or commanded. Love depends on free will. When God created us, He created us in His image. He gave us the ability to love, to create, to make moral judgments, to choose, to think, to worship. God's intention for humans was, and is, for us to be in relationship with Him, a relationship not of fear but of love. Sadly, however, the first humans immediately used their free will to turn away from God's love, and hid when they heard His voice. They abused free will, and sin entered the world.

Some then argue that God must have known that this was what

humans would do with free will. And they would be right about that. But, while God knew what we would do with our free will from the beginning, He also, from the beginning, was preparing the way for the sending of His only Son into the world in order that we might be restored into a love-relationship with Him. The choice to turn to Jesus and to receive salvation is as open to us as refusing even to acknowledge Him. It *has* to be by free will and not by force or control. This means that those who have accepted God's offer of love in Christ, through the cross, have entered an eternal fellowship of love. They are related now to the Father by love, as beloved children. They are part of the family that will be gathered together with the Father eternally.

*   *   *   *   *

Many take the line that God should always prevent the death of a child, stop the bullet, kill off all dictators, turn the boiling water cold before it scalds, slam on the brakes of the runaway lorry, render the rapist impotent, remove sexual desire from the paedophile, make drunk drivers lose their car keys, stop the bomb plot, prevent all diseases, cause the knife in the hand of the stabber to turn to putty, or neutralise the gas chambers of the Holocaust. Although there are occasions when it seems God has intervened in an out-of-the-ordinary way, if this were universally the case then life would be more or less impossible, as nothing would be predictable. It would reduce the world to confusion. D.Λ. Carson writes: 'That God normally operates the universe consistently makes science possible; that he does not always do so ought to keep science humble.'[3] Free will also needs a consistent world in which to operate and make choices.

Does being omnipotent mean that God can do anything? Is He really the Sovereign God of the universe? Yes, He is, and can do anything physically, but not anything that is illogical – for instance, He cannot make a quadrangle into a triangle; a single shape cannot be both. It would be self-contradictory. So, apart from illogical actions, can God really do anything? Dr Alister McGrath writes:

> Could he command someone to hate him, for example? A quick
> check suggests that there is no logical contradiction here. But
> there seems to be something terribly wrong. Although there is no
> contradiction within the statement itself, it seems to fly in the
> face of everything we know about God. It is not logic but basic
> Christianity that is offended. The problem is not internal (with
> the logic) but external (with the view of God it implies).[4]

Similarly, if we ask the question, 'Can God break his promises?' we
see the issue is not about power but about character. As Dr McGrath
points out:

> There are things that God could do that God would not do —
> again, emphasising the issue of God's character. If God could do
> anything he liked, he would be whimsical and capricious. The
> Bible speaks to us of a God who is faithful to his promises, and
> who enters into a covenant with his people. That means he stands
> by his promises!

Thus, although God is sovereign, and could give humans free will and
then withhold it whenever He willed, this would not be true to His
character as God. Human rebellion at the beginning was not His will, but
rather the exercise of free will by our first ancestors. Omnipotence could
only have stopped it by withdrawing free will entirely from humanity.
It follows that God is grieved to see the mess we make of His world; that
He is deeply saddened by the early death of a teenage driver in a head-on
car crash; that His heart is broken over the wars, the refugees and the
poor. It is not the sort of world He desires us to inhabit.

Yet, even though free will can bring about some terrible
consequences as well as causing so many wonderful things to happen
in the world, God's sovereignty is still over all. He has seen the end
from the beginning. Although human free will affects the details of
life on earth, our Sovereign God's actions and purposes are never
absolutely dependent on human actions. He does, in Scripture, choose
to 'relent', or to alter His mind in response to 'conversing' with His

people, or as a response to their prayers (see Exod. 32:14, where God relents after Moses' passionate pleading), but He can never be *forced* to do so, and His overall will and purpose can never be stopped by human action. Indeed, His purposes are being worked out both in spite of and because of our free will. Ephesians 1:11 speaks of 'the plan of him who works out everything in conformity with the purpose of his will, in order that we ... might be for the praise of his glory.' When, by free will and love, we desire to glorify Him in our lives, we can be part of His purposes. We can also rest on the truth that His eternal will cannot be thwarted; His eternal purposes will be fulfilled.

Often when Romans 8:28 is quoted ('in all things God works for the good of those who love him ...'), the second half of the verse ('who have been called according to his purpose') is left out. As a result, the verse is frequently misused for our personal good (even in order to find a parking place!), whereas it is actually referring to *God's* good purpose. Philippians 2:12–13 spells it out: '... continue to work out your salvation with fear and trembling, for it is God who works in you to will and to act according to his good purpose' (italics mine). One friend who found the idea of God's omnipotence hard to take in the light of her suffering, eventually realised that His omnipotence was being worked out through her suffering.

There are many examples of God intervening for His purposes in history and in personal lives. We see this in the Bible, in our lives and in churches, and these are just the occasions that we know about. Usually these interventions are special hugs of encouragement for His children, or moments when He chooses to remind us that He is God (even by acting through unbelievers), or when He has a special purpose to fulfil through us. Many of us can reflect on a large number of occasions when there seems no other explanation but that God has intervened ... for His purposes.

As much as we have abused free will, it is still a wonderful gift to humanity. For all who belong to Christ, the exercise of our free will should increasingly be for good, truth, integrity, love, meaning, fulfilment, justice, care and mercy, to be more and more the sort of humans God intended us to be, and to do His will. At the same time, we should stand against those who choose evil, hatred, bitterness, conflict, greed, crime, materialism, immorality, and all forms of godlessness. The Holy Spirit gives us the strength to make these choices, even though we must disappoint Him so many times. Of course, free will can be used for good, by those who do not follow Christ but, when we become Christians, the choices we make are also evidence of a genuine relationship with Him.

C.S. Lewis writes:

The Christian doctrine of suffering explains, I believe, a very curious fact about the world we live in. The settled happiness and security which we all desire, God withholds from us by the very nature of the world: but joy, happiness and merriment, He has scattered broadcast. We are never safe, but we have plenty of fun, and some ecstasy ... Our Father refreshes us on the journey with some pleasant inns, but will not encourage us to mistake them for home.[5]

NOTES

1   William Hazlitt, *Essays* (London: Walter Scott, 1889), p.269.
2   Broadcast sermon, 4 September 2009.
3   D.A. Carson *How Long, O Lord?* (Leicester: IVP, 1982), p.243.
4   From a letter by Dr Alister McGrath to assist me on this theme. I am grateful for his further help and input.
5   C.S. Lewis, *The Problem of Pain*, copyright © C.S. Lewis Pte. Limited, 1941. Extract reprinted by permission.

THREE

Why doesn't God stop all wars, crimes and evil?

'If you'd been in the trenches in the First World War you wouldn't believe in God either.' Jim had always avoided contact with me as rector of the parish, although his wife was a lovely Christian and a member of our church. She had told me that he said those words repeatedly. Now he had accidentally bumped into me. The words came out like a recorded announcement on a train. 'Jim,' I said, 'I have seen a great number of photographic records, read many first-hand accounts and have seen the reconstructions in the Imperial War Museum, making me hurry outside before I was sick. But surely, that war should have made you cease to believe in man, not God?' The horrors of 'the war to end all wars' came about through human decisions and actions, the generals sitting safely well back from the front line ordering tens of thousands of men into the teeth of the machine guns and almost certain death – the slaughter of so many men to achieve a few yards of ground. Most of that was human folly and a callous disregard for the value of human life.

The year of that contact with Jim was 1968, half a century after the war that had scarred him so deeply had ended, and the block against God had been in Jim's ears all that time. To his wife's delight (and mine!), Jim could finally see the point, and returned to the faith and to being part of the church.

Sadly, when people say, after some act of kindness, 'it has restored my faith in human nature', you know that restoration will not last! Human nature can rise to astonishing heights of good, but also sink to abhorrent depths. It was this paradox of human nature that drew the prominent social philosopher, C.E.M. Joad, to the Christian faith. During the late 1940s, he was known throughout Britain because of his penetrating style of answering in the radio series *The Brains Trust*. His turning to Christianity shocked his fellow philosophers and the nation. The reason for his conversion, he said, was that no other philosophy explained human nature. The Christian faith showed that humans were made in the image of God with so much potential for creativity and good, but had also fallen into rebellion against God, and this explained the many manifestations of sin and evil. He said that none of the socialist schemes, aimed at bringing in a utopian society, had ever succeeded because of one factor – human nature. Professor Joad saw the rejection of the doctrine of original sin by those in the more left-wing political arena of his day as having resulted in what he called 'the shallow optimism in regard to human nature', which meant that they were 'always being disappointed' when their great new society never came to pass.[1]

When human free will is nurtured by love and goodness, it is wonderful. Yet when it is nurtured by self-interest, by material greed, and by the desire for power, the results have a terrible impact on so many other human lives. Sin is putting 'self' first, in the place of God. From the first moment our earliest ancestors listened to Satan[2] rather than God, sin began to reign in human lives as well as affecting the earth (see Gen. 3). Satan's whole aim is to separate us from God. Romans 1:18–32 vividly describes the consequences of refusing to honour God or give thanks to Him: '[we] ... exchanged the truth of God for a lie ... changed natural relations for unnatural ones ... [and have] become filled with every kind of wickedness ... senseless, faithless, heartless, ruthless ...'

The sickening aspects of human sin and evil, therefore, are the result of seeking to live without God. At the national and world level this has always been so, and if we only look back across the last one hundred years we see it in stark awfulness. We saw it in the rise of the Nazi regime under power-mad Hitler, the doctrine of domination, the desire for world power, the obscene principle that the world needed to be 'cleansed' of all Jews, resulting in the horrific Holocaust. We saw it in the murderous regime of Stalin. We saw it in the killing fields of Cambodia under the ruthless Pol Pot regime. We see it in the appalling state of the people of Zimbabwe due to the megalomania of Mugabe. We recall the terror wrought by Idi Amin in Uganda. We see it in civil wars, and in terrorist atrocities committed in the name of religion. We hear of the Taliban stopping all female education, beheading their opponents, exerting horrendous controls on their own people to restrict their freedom. We rightly call these terrible abuses of power 'satanic'. Our minds reel at the statistics of the numbers who are refugees. We are told by the charity World Vision that more than 26,000 children *a day* die of starvation or of a disease that could have been prevented.

The cry 'Why doesn't God stop it?' was considered in the previous chapter. We either have a world of total control, or a world where humans are given freedom. The fact that free will can be so abused, as well as so wonderfully used, is part of the consequence.

As Alan Greenspan, the former chairman of the Federal Reserve in the USA, was reported as saying, 'Unless someone can change human nature, we will have more human crises.'[3] That could just be the charter for a world mission to bring people to Christ, for only through Him can we see human nature being changed, by the Holy Spirit. The promise of Jeremiah 31:33 'I will put my law in their minds and write it on their hearts. I will be their God, and they will be my people' was fulfilled through Christ and by the power of the Holy Spirit. Jesus said: '... no-one can enter the kingdom of God unless he is born of water and the Spirit. Flesh gives birth to flesh, but the Spirit gives birth to spirit. You should not be surprised at my saying, "You must be born again"' (John 3:5–7).

If anyone thinks that atheism is the answer to all our problems, they should read the book *Mao: The Unknown Story*.[4] So dreadful was Mao's lust for power and so total was his disregard for the value of human life, it takes great resolve to read it, but only by doing so do we get the full view of the depths of atheistic evil.[5] Unsurprisingly, Mao dismissed any form of commandments. All considerations must 'be purely calculation for oneself, and absolutely not for obeying external ethical codes, or for so-called feelings of responsibility ...'[6] Those opposing him were put to death in dreadful ways. And just to make sure the populace knew exactly what was expected of them, he wrote his ideas down in his little red book, *Thoughts of Chairman Mao*.

At the level of most people's lives, we can see human sin and the abuse of free will in the drunken driver, the greed of some bankers causing the world credit crunch, gang violence, drug trafficking and addiction, cheating in sport, corruption in some political leaders, the callous treatment of other human beings that produces emotional or physical damage, the terrorism that can crash planes into the Twin Towers and murder thousands of innocent people in the name of religion, the oppression that drives large numbers of people from their homes into refugee camps and devastating poverty ... The list could go on and on.

Christ is the key to delivering us from sin and changing our lives and our world, if we would let Him do so. John 1:4–6 reads: 'In him was life, and that life was the light of men. The light shines in the darkness, but the darkness has not understood [overcome] it.' The rejection of Christ as the Light is vividly described in John 3:19–21:

> 'This is the verdict: Light has come into the world, but men loved darkness instead of light because their deeds were evil. Everyone who does evil hates the light, and will not come into the light for fear that his deeds will be exposed. But whoever lives by the truth comes into the light, so that it may be seen plainly that what he has done has been done through God.'

In the summer of 2009, the Archbishop of Canterbury arranged a debate on 'The contribution of science and faith to a society that values understanding'. In it, Dr Conor Cunningham, Assistant Director of the Centre of Philosophy at Nottingham University, argued that the nihilistic philosophy of a Dawkins-esque universe is dangerous: 'The banishment of God, something enabled by the strict opposition of the natural and the unnatural' (a debate he earlier describes as false, irrelevant and nonsensical) 'has come at an enormous cost. We have ended up in a world, a supposedly natural world that is devoid of that which we presume to be natural: people, free will, first-person language, colour, ethics, organisms, and indeed life itself.' He quoted the words of several philosophers:

> 'Could it turn out that no one has believed anything?'

> 'No such thing as selves exists in the world: Nobody ever was or had a self.'

> 'Ethics is an illusion fobbed off on us by our genes.'

> 'There is no longer plain right and plain wrong. The ideological exclusion of the importance of religion is indeed the beginning of reality's destruction.'[7]

In the light of that awful scenario, I am the more thankful that I came to know Christ as my Saviour, the One who died for my sins on the cross to bring me forgiveness, and as my Lord – Lord of all, including my life – more than fifty years ago. During that time, I have become ever more convinced that the Bible is the key to understanding humanity, the world, life itself. It makes sense. I have also come to realise increasingly that the only answer to changing lives is through Christ, and that the truth and relevance of His Word is the best guide for how to live in this world. Paul challenges us: 'Live as children of light (for the fruit of the light consists in all goodness, righteousness and truth) and find out what pleases the Lord' (Eph. 5:8–10).

With the world as it is, humans may feel better (and relieved of responsibility) if they blame God for sin and evil, but only by turning to God in Christ will they find help, forgiveness, meaning, purpose, transformation and hope.

NOTES

1   C.E.M. Joad expressed these views in *The Recovery of Belief* (London: Faber & Faber, 1952). The book was about his return to the Christian faith, a faith he had rejected as an undergraduate. It was published a year before his death. See note 1 in Chapter 1.

2   The serpent of Genesis 3 is named as Satan in Revelation 12:9.

3   *The Times*, 11 September 2009.

4   Jung Chang and Jon Halliday, *Mao: The Unknown Story* (London: Jonathan Cape, 2005). Used by permission of the Random House Group Limited and Aitken Alexander Associates Limited.

5   The book *Mao: The Unknown Story* shows Mao's callous indifference to human suffering. His policy of taking agricultural produce to sell abroad in order to get money for an atomic bomb was the main cause of 38 million people dying of starvation when famine came in the period 1958–61 (p.456). His ruthless purges and his lust for personal power showed rampant evil.

6   Ibid. pp.13–14.

7   I am grateful for Dr Cunningham's permission to quote freely from his notes.

FOUR

Why is there *in*justice
if God is a God of justice?

'For those of us who started out as Christians, flirted with atheism and ended up as doubters, the question of a merciful God is a pretty big one. Indeed, for many it is the killer question', writes John Humphrys.[1] 'We are told that faith, goodness and virtue are always rewarded and that wickedness will be punished', he continues. And then, throwing down the gauntlet, he remarks, 'Then we look around us and what do we see? Precisely the opposite.' Michael Buerk, the award-winning broadcaster who was acclaimed for bringing the terrible famine in Ethiopia in 1984–85 to the world's notice, said that this had caused him to lose faith in God, as it demonstrated the terrible injustice (such as the suffering of the innocent) in the world.

So, once again, we have this requirement of a God who constantly intervenes, righting wrongs everywhere, bringing justice and judgment, sorting out the mess humanity has made. He is a God whom we can apparently ignore, but who is there to make the world fair and just. We would presumably expect such a God to level the wealth of all people so that, for example, the bankers would not be able to award themselves huge bonuses, the rich would lose their yachts, there would be no first class on the transport systems, and successful broadcasters on high salaries would have their income cut drastically, as the money would be needed in the refugee camps of Africa and the Middle East. Our world would be so *controlled* if justice really was meted out by God in this way.

We have to ask the question, once again, 'Do we really want to be controlled, or would we prefer to have free will?' God graciously granted us free will to enable us to make our own choices. We abused that gift by choosing to sin. This in turn has led to all the injustices we see in the world today. In other words, unfairness is our fault, not God's.

In response to John Humphrys' statement that 'we are told' that 'faith, goodness and virtue are always rewarded and that wickedness will be punished', we respond: 'Who told you?' It is certainly a concept in popular thinking: 'This is my reward for doing something good' or 'My punishment for doing something wrong' ('What have I done to deserve this?'). It sounds as if God is a schoolmaster, with reward points in one hand and a cane in the other.

One correspondent wrote this to me: 'I saw a very great deal of the most awful suffering, the brunt of it falling on those – young children, for instance – who were obviously innocent of any kind of "sin".' As a Christian, I am sickened at the very suggestion of such a judgmental God.

Such ideas perhaps come from an experience of 'fear-religion', a concept of God keeping a stern eye on our every word and deed. But this is not a religion that I recognise from the New Testament. Faith, goodness and virtue are not requirements for reward, although they do bring about the blessing of living more in harmony with God and the rest of God's children. Yes, in the Old Testament there is a lot said about judgment and discipline, and there are promises made of specific blessing (eg the quiver full of children, the good harvest), but they are almost always for encouraging or disciplining the people of God as a whole community. In the New Testament, however, we move into the fuller revelation of God through Jesus Christ, where love and mercy dominate. This is dramatically shown in the incident of the woman caught in the act of adultery in John 8:7–11 where the judgmental law of the Old Testament is overturned by our Lord with understanding and forgiveness, even though He still tells the woman not to sin in the same way again.

In the New Testament, most references to punishment are in relation to the earthly authorities (Rom. 13:4–5) and the Church (2 Cor. 2:6), with the notable exception being the final judgment. As for the notion of reward, this is mostly considered in terms of heaven: '... because great is your reward in heaven', Jesus says in Luke 6:23, and Moses 'was looking ahead to his reward' in Hebrews 11:26. In this life, our principal reward is knowing that we do God's will, especially in sharing the gospel (1 Cor. 9:18). As Ignatius of Loyola puts it:

> *So teach us, Lord, to serve Thee as Thou deservest, to give and not to count the cost, to fight and not to heed the wounds, to toil and not to seek for rest, to labour and not to ask for any reward save that of knowing that we do Thy will.*

The injustices of the world *are* terrible – the oppression of innocent people, the imprisonment and torture of any who speak out against the ruling authority, the forcing of millions from their homes into refugee camps, the lack of human rights and so much more – but accusations have to be against humans, not against God.

There is nothing new in feeling let down by God over justice, or questioning whether God cares about justice. A young man at a party tackled me with such a charge: 'I seek to do good, doing what is right and living a godly life, yet I am facing many problems; my unbelieving friends snap their fingers at the law, live for themselves, do not care about others and have success and money. It isn't fair. Isn't God supposed to bring justice?' To his surprise, I told him he was not the first person to think like that! I took out my New Testament and Psalms, and suggested he read Psalm 73. He was amazed to discover that the psalmist felt just what he felt. For twelve verses he speaks of the arrogance of the wicked in their prosperity, their good health, their pride and violence, their callousness and evil conceits, and their challenge to God. The psalmist then cries, 'Surely in vain have I kept my heart pure', and feels he is being punished. Then, in verse 17, everything changes. He enters the sanctuary of God and understands that the final destiny of the wicked is to be cast down and destroyed, and at the same time he sees afresh that God is with him, holding him, guiding him, and afterwards will take him to glory. Yes, his flesh and heart may fail, but God is the strength of his heart and his portion, for *ever*. The psalmist realises that the question of justice and judgment is to be settled in the future, when life on earth comes to an end. Meanwhile, he takes comfort in what the unbeliever cannot know – he has God with him.

In the same vein, the prophet Habakkuk (Hab. 1:2) complains, 'How long, O LORD, must I call for help, but you do not listen?' remarking in verse 4 of chapter 1 that 'The wicked hem in the righteous, so that justice is perverted'. In the end, however, God convinces him that they are marked for judgment (Hab. 2) so that Habakkuk can exult in the Lord (Hab. 3:18).

The desire to see judgment – revenge – brought on others is a 'natural' reaction. In the final moments of a recent episode of a popular TV soap, a sinister-faced man was given the line: 'I'm going to make sure that every member of his family suffers for what he did.' This passion for revenge leads to family break-up, to gang warfare, to civil war, to war between nations. Time and time again we hear such actions supported by the phrase 'an eye for an eye, a tooth for a tooth'. But that phrase, from the Old Testament, was intended to put a limit on revenge, not to give permission for unbridled vengeance. This idea, though, was smashed 2,000 years ago by Jesus Christ, when He said, 'But I tell you, Do not resist an evil person. If someone strikes you on the right cheek, turn to him the other also' (see Matt. 5:38–42). The notion is reaffirmed in Romans 12:17–21, where Paul tells believers not to take revenge, to leave the righting of injustices to God on Judgment Day, as we, meanwhile, overcome evil with good. When the Scottish justice minister made his much-maligned decision to release the Libyan aircraft bomber, al-Megrahi, on compassionate grounds in 2009, he was reported as saying, '… there are those who fail to recognise that there is a New Testament as well as an Old Testament'.

For Christians, the injustices of the world cause agony of heart and deep compassion. We know that most injustice is due to man's inhumanity to man. We do not blame God. Yet, as we see the growing gap between rich and poor, the vast shanty towns in parts of the world, the intolerable living conditions of the street people (as harrowingly portrayed in the film *Slumdog Millionaire*), the sites of concentration camps, the refugee camps, those dying of hunger, the devastation of lives caused by power-mad dictators and repressive regimes, we can have only one response: 'What can we do to help redress this injustice?'

That is how the mercy of God operates – through us.

Bob Geldof stirred the nation about the needs of the world. Michael Buerk made us face up to injustice when he exposed the suffering in Ethiopia in the 1980s, and started the flow of billions of pounds in aid to save millions of lives. He did not do it as a Christian. However, it was exactly in line with what our just God asks of us, to right wrongs, feed the needy, and bring justice. Tearfund's Sara Shaw well expressed the Christian concern for justice when she said, 'Helping people adapt is an issue of justice. Poor people didn't cause climate change, but they are the hardest hit by it. We have a responsibility to help them adapt.'

The need for God's people to act with justice runs through the Old Testament:

The Law	'… do not pervert justice by siding with the crowd' (Exod. 23:2). 'Do not deny justice to your poor people in their lawsuits' (Exod. 23:6). 'Do not pervert justice or show partiality … Follow justice, and justice alone' (Deut. 16:19–20).
Job	A sense of injustice from God runs through the book of Job. Job begins by seeing the world with himself at the centre, but in the end sees it with God at the centre, as when God says, in Job 40:8, 'Would you discredit my justice?'
The Psalms	The psalmists cry out for justice now, but mostly rejoice in God's final justice.
The Prophets	All the prophets are concerned about justice. The leading champion was Amos, with his concerns for justice in the courts for the poor, and his attack on those who denied justice to the oppressed (Amos 2:7; 5:7). It is Amos who says (in Amos 5) that God hates their religious assemblies because they do not have concern for justice, and he gives God's word: 'let justice roll on like a river, righteousness like a never-failing stream' (v.24).

In the New Testament, our Lord's teaching in the Sermon on the Mount (Matt. 5–7) is a charter for righteous living, and His concern for the oppressed, the outcasts, the lepers, the blind, deaf, dumb, the wounded (in the story of the Good Samaritan in Luke 10:25–37), the mentally disturbed and those needing food, challenges us to do likewise in this present world. Jesus condemns those who neglect justice, mercy and faithfulness (Matt. 23:23). Although the primary thrust of the New Testament is to show that Jesus is the Son of God, and to teach and explain the purpose of the cross as the place where God's justice and love meet in the Son of God dying for our sins that we might be justified – made right with God – it is also about building a kingdom of renewed people who will seek to live just and holy lives. That includes being concerned for justice, which William Temple called God's 'love in action'.

James, as head of the Jerusalem church, fought hard to stop injustices and to bring justice to the city. In his letter he condemns favouritism in the courts, the way the poor are humiliated, the people who say they believe but have no mercy or practical action to the needy, the failure of the rich to pay proper wages while they themselves wallow in wealth, and the condemning and murdering of innocent men. In James 2:13, he exclaims, 'mercy triumphs over judgement!' No wonder the authorities arranged for James to be assassinated. He stood for justice in the name of his God, the God of justice, earning him the nickname 'James the Just'.

Nevertheless, the ultimate justice by our righteous God is in the final judgment. There, at last, all the injustices of this world will be exposed and judged. Paul says in Acts 17:31 that God 'has set a day when he will judge the world with justice by the man he has appointed.' Revelation 20:11–15 says that the final judgment will be the day when right will be rewarded and wrong will be condemned, when the heart-cry to the God of justice and mercy will be fully answered. Miroslav Volf writes: 'A non-indignant God would be an accomplice in injustice, deception and violence'.[2] A young man said to me recently: 'If I did not think there would be a Day of Reckoning, I would give up.' The old accusation that Christians are only interested in 'pie in the sky when you die', and thus not concerned for the needs of this world, is far from the truth. The opposite applies. That hope inspires us to do everything we can to meet those needs, and that includes seeking to bring justice in this world.

All this poses a question for those who query our faith: 'You talk about justice, but where did the idea of justice come from?' If humans are just animals, then one look at the animal world shows not a whiff of justice, only the survival of the most powerful. The amazing natural history programmes we see on our TV screens spare us little detail – consider, for example, a 'cute' young penguin being eaten by a seal, and that same seal being preyed on by a killer whale. Nobody has told the animal kingdom about justice! So, if humans are animals, why hasn't evolution led to only the fittest and most powerful surviving in our race, the haves getting more and the have-nots getting less? And why should we be concerned about justice?

In his Presidential Address to the British Science Association in September 2009, Lord May spoke about Darwin's three big problems. Two, he said, are solved, but one has never been solved: 'explaining how cooperative or altruistic behaviour among animals evolved.' It goes against the survival of the fittest. Despite being an atheist, he was of the opinion that, to bring co-operation over global warming and world food supplies, we needed a religion or even an omnipotent deity to dole out punishment.[3] His belief system would presumably not allow him to consider that human beings are more than animals, and are endowed with the image of God, which includes justice. It would certainly solve the problem for him. So how did we come to develop the whole Western legal tradition, a tradition that is renowned for its fairness? Many Greek and Roman philosophers saw justice as an inherent natural right, but there is no such natural right for animals, so there must be something very distinctive about humans – which is what the Bible teaches, of course. Others think that justice is a purely human creation, which means we can alter the concept as we wish. The prospects of that are terrifying.

Christians believe justice to be rooted in God, and would maintain that most rules of justice in the West have been honed by Scripture.

Charles Colson writes: '... only a biblical worldview can produce true justice. For justice is impossible without the rule of law and the rule of law is impossible without transcendent authority.' Does this explain why justice is so difficult to get in some countries? Colson continues: '... the whole Western legal tradition has been profoundly shaped by and remains influenced by powerful Christian ideas and themes.'[4] It is, we suggest, only because God has revealed Himself and shown us what He expects of humanity that we have any understanding of, or will for, justice. It springs from Him – the God of justice and mercy.

Baroness Caroline Cox is an outstanding Christian. It is because of that living faith that her action for those suffering injustice in the world is so bold, enterprising, effective and compassionate. In particular, she champions the cause of those parts of the world usually overlooked by the international media, such as the Armenian enclave of Nagorno Karabakh, relocated by Stalin in Azerbaijan, west and east Burma, southern Sudan, Nigeria, northern Uganda, Timor Leste. Her Relief Organisation[5] operates by asking the people in those areas to choose and be responsible for the programmes they support. The target is always the people who are disregarded by the world, under oppression or being persecuted. She gives herself by travelling constantly to these areas. She is an advocate for human rights in Burma, and is trying to help improve the relations between North and South Korea. All this, and yet campaigning in the UK for disabled rights and so much else! Lady Cox is a champion of the victims of injustice. She does not blame God; she knows it is humans who are to blame, but she acts as a servant of our righteous God to make a difference. She also urges all Christian believers to be involved wherever they can, both in the needs elsewhere in the world but also in their own neighbourhood in the needs of their area ... hospices, hostels for the homeless, the social disparities and so on. So where is the God of justice and mercy? Right here!

NOTES

1   John Humphrys, In God We Doubt (London: Hodder & Stoughton, 2007), p.137.
     Reproduced by permission of Hodder and Stoughton Limited.
2   Miroslav Volf, Exclusion and Embrace (Nashville, TN: Abingdon Press, 1996), p.297.
3   Robert, Professor Lord May of Oxford, OM AC FRS. The paper was entitled: 'The Evolution
     of Cooperation: Darwin's unsolved problem and its relevance to environmental concerns'.
     I am grateful to Lord May for allowing me to quote from his script.
4   Charles Colson, from his London Lectures in 2000 at All Souls, Langham Place, London,
     entitled 'Justice that Restores', pp.13–45. Quoted by kind permission of Charles Colson
     and Prison Fellowship Ministries, www.pfm.org. Charles ('Chuck') Colson was Special
     Counsel for President Richard Nixon, 1969–73. Since his prison sentence, he has brought his
     Christian faith to bear in a lifetime commitment to his Prison Fellowship Ministries in 100
     countries, and to reforming the criminal justice system in the light of Christian principles.
5   Humanitarian Aid Relief Trust – www.hart-uk.org. My sincere thanks to Baroness Cox.

FIVE

Why has this happened to me – what have I done to deserve this?

'My wife has been to church every Sunday all her life, and now she has this cancer. What has she done to deserve this?'

'I prayed that my son would come back from the war. He didn't. Why has this happened to me?'

'She was a marvellous worker for Christian causes, and yet dropped dead at twenty-eight. She was my only daughter. Why?'

Two youngsters contract the same disease at the same time. They are both prayed for. One survives. One doesn't. 'Why has this happened to us?' cry the bereaved parents.

The university undergraduate suddenly hangs himself, and leaves a note on a social networking site: 'Who would I like to meet? God, to ask him what I've done wrong.'

'Seeing my beloved relative deteriorating into incontinence and the indignities associated with it is sickening. I prayed and he got worse. Why has God inflicted this on him? I thought God was merciful.'

At funerals, by the bedside of many ill people, numerous versions of the same question are expressed. For many, this is the end of faith in God.

The question arises from the view, widely held, of God being someone who causes good and bad things to happen according to our deeds.

In the dramatic book of Job, it is Job's friends who persist in the belief that Job's sufferings must be deserved and so he should repent. Yet we are shown that none of the suffering is caused by God; it is caused by Satan, to challenge the reality of Job's faith in God. It presses the point that real faith will hold on to God and it exposes the 'What have you done to deserve this?' thinking. However, the book also wrestles with the reality of deep and raw suffering, the sense of being let down and even abandoned. Job was convinced he was innocent, and the way his friends came up with reasons and answers only exacerbated the situation. Job's heart cry was real, although the idea that it was God who doled out the suffering was wrong. So, whenever we try to point out the falsity of asking 'What have I done to deserve this?' we also need to have real sympathy for the sufferer, so often feeling deep emotional pain.

We get even nearer the unfathomable depths of suffering when we hear our Lord, on the cross, cry out the first line of Psalm 22: 'My God, my God, why have you forsaken me?' For the psalmist, it was the feeling of God-forsakenness which hurt most of all (and this has been so for many believers ever since). For our Lord, the depth of God-forsakenness He experienced was infinitely greater because it was not due to physical suffering, but because He was bearing the sins of the world and the resulting separation from God. If ever we feel we are forsaken by God, we can know that Christ understands because He experienced it beyond anything we can imagine. Yet, even in the greatest depths of feeling God's absence, God was and is there.

In the New Testament, this idea about some suffering being deserved persists, but it is *emphatically denied* by Christ. In John 9:1–3, when His disciples asked Him, regarding the man born blind from birth, 'who sinned, this man or his parents, that he was born blind?' Jesus answered, 'Neither this man nor his parents sinned.' In Luke 13:1–5, Jesus shows that *anyone* may become caught up in the arbitrary happenings of life: 'Do you think that these Galileans were worse sinners than all the other Galileans because they suffered this way?' He asks, referring to the latest 'gossip' that Pilate had mixed the Galileans' blood with their sacrifices. He then continues, 'Or those eighteen who died when the tower in Siloam fell on them – do you think they were more guilty than all the others living in Jerusalem?'

Returning to the present day, Frances Young, in her book *Face to Face*[1] tells of the driver of a hired minibus, picking up handicapped children, asking, 'What on earth have the parents done to have children like these?' Equally unbelievable was when someone said to a family, distraught at the loss of their child, 'So God slapped you down' and 'God disciplines those whom he loves'. The idea that God caused the child's death as discipline is appalling, and is aeons away from the God we know in Christ.

Consider also another tragic and awful accident that devastated a whole family. The sinful carelessness of the driver who crashed his vehicle into the family, the suddenness and the trauma of death, limb loss and various other injuries evoked the sympathy and horror of all who heard about it. A couple of years later, we learnt that before the accident they had been regular churchgoers, but now they had faltered in their churchgoing because they wondered what they had done wrong 'to deserve this'. My sadness for them was compounded by that statement. Somehow the view of God they had before the accident was verging towards a God who rewards or punishes. They needed to see that what happened was sheer sin on the part of the driver, and that it was utterly random that they were hit. This is the fallen world in which we live. Once we understand that and stop blaming God, we can throw ourselves back into the arms of God and His abounding love. To reject Him is to reject the only One who can really help us.

The question 'What have I done to deserve this?' can become personally destructive. The nagging feeling that *we* have caused this tragedy or illness to happen by some action or inaction turns into a feeling of guilt which gnaws away at our hearts and minds for years – even for life. It wears down the spirit and blocks our being able to start afresh and go on positively with life. So the quicker we face it and dismiss it, the better.

It happens to believers too. A lady wrote to thank me after I had preached on suffering and healing. She said: 'You have removed my guilt. I am involved in a ministry of healing to other people, but have felt guilty that I am not healed of my own illness.' The guilt sprang from the false idea given to her that if you are not healed as a Christian, you must have hidden sin or lack of faith. Our God is *emphatically* NOT a God who acts like that to believers or unbelievers.

It is true that God does discipline His children, like any loving parent (Heb. 12:4–11), but only to produce better lives. As Christians, instead of asking the question, 'What have I done to deserve this?', we should be asking, 'What is God helping me to learn from this?', and when we are caught up in, and wounded by, the sins of the world, consider 'How can I handle this for God's glory?'

Prebendary John Skinner[2] told me of a memorable afternoon in his parochial ministry. He went to a local hospital to visit a Merchant Navy man who lived in the parish, but was not a churchgoer. The ward was a long one, with ladies at one end and men at the other. As John walked into the ward, the Merchant Navy man saw his clerical collar and immediately burst out with rage: 'Why has God allowed this to happen to me? I've always been fit and never had an illness in my life, and now this has happened!' John said what he could, but it was almost impossible for the man to hear anything, such was his anger with God. John then moved down to the end of the ward where there was a lovely, godly, much-loved elderly lady in her eighties, who was a wonderful member of the church and now a patient in this ward. She used almost the same words, but in an entirely different tone of voice to the navy man. She also said, but quietly and thoughtfully, 'Why has God allowed this to happen to me?' For her, the question was not one of querying God, but of wanting to know what His will was for her in ministry there, and to whom, in particular, she should give most care. That was what she was doing. Wearing her dressing gown, she went from bed to bed with a beaming face of love and friendship, and ministered to all.

NOTES
1 Frances Young, *Face to Face* (London: Epworth Press, 1985), p.58.
2 I am grateful to Prebendary John Skinner for this quote.

SIX

Why doesn't God prevent 'natural' disasters?

On 26 December 2004, an enormous undersea earthquake occurred in the Indian Ocean. The resulting 30-metre-high tidal wave or tsunami swept across several countries, causing massive destruction. Some 230,000 people were killed, and millions more were made homeless, bringing about a huge humanitarian response. The catastrophe also led a large number of people (even Christian believers) to blame God, to challenge the idea of His being merciful, or to abandon their faith in Him.

When the tides of emotion began to recede, the 'charge' against God needed to be answered.

Most 'natural' disasters evoke a similar charge. It was immediately made on the BBC *Today* programme, when the appalling earthquake devastated part of Haiti in January 2010; there was an enormous death toll in that impoverished country. For those caught up in such disasters there is trauma, fear, despair and often anger. These days, most other people in the world are also able to see and respond to what has happened through television coverage which brings the stark realities of the terrible results of earthquakes, hurricanes and floods into our living rooms. Sympathy, heartache, contributing to the relief fund ... we all become involved.

As we think about this we need, first, to be realistic about the amazing world in which we live. The paralysis of European air travel for six days in April 2010 due to the ash from one volcano erupting in Iceland was a sharp reminder that the earth is not some stainless steel box of perfection, but a planet revolving in space amongst millions of other planets, affected by the sun, the moon, the universe itself. Scientists tell us that the earth's core, some 4,000 miles beneath the surface, is solid iron surrounded by extremely hot molten iron, estimated at between 5,000 and 11,000°F! According to the theory of the Big Bang, the universe not only expanded from a very dense and very hot state, but *continues to expand*, right up to the present day. Indeed, we are told that space itself is expanding, carrying galaxies with it. And our world is part of it all!

It is the movement of tectonic plates that causes earthquakes (the country of Haiti was actually formed by a collision of plates). It is also their movement through which an earth able to sustain life was formed. They have been and remain a crucial factor in the development of civilisations, bringing many benefits for life, such as enabling us to access water beneath the desert, or to find oil and minerals, or in the way they brought copper to the surface and made it possible for us to make bronze and iron. They are essential for the ongoing renewal of the earth, and therefore of life.[1] We only call them 'disasters' when they harm human life and property.

Dr Alister McGrath writes: 'The existence of carbon-based life on Earth depends upon a delicate balance of physical and cosmological forces and parameters, which are such that were any one of these quantities to be slightly altered, *the balance would be destroyed and life would not exist*' (italics mine).[2]

So do we still want to charge God with allowing their movements to happen? Could He have provided life some other way to avoid earthquakes happening? That is beyond our minds to know. Christians trust His wisdom that what we have in this amazing universe is the best way of providing and *sustaining* life.

Nevertheless, as we are only too aware, the plate movements will also continue to cause earthquakes. If we live on top of one of the fault lines between plates, now that we know where they are, we take a risk (especially if we do not build responsibly), but can hardly blame God when the plates move and clash, causing earthquakes and tsunamis – unless we want to blame Him for the way the whole universe was made and exists.

The tectonic plates of Eurasia and America are moving very slowly *apart* by a few centimetres each year, causing volcanic eruptions.

This Mid-Atlantic Ridge is particularly visible in Iceland, the only land where these plates meet and the rift valley created between the plates is dramatically visible. (The Icelanders also benefit from the vast underground heat which powers most homes and industries.) The San Andreas Fault in California is very visible to the eye. In the huge Pacific Ring of Fire (on which 452 volcanoes are situated), running from north-east of Australia through the islands by the equator, including Indonesia, up through China and Japan, and then down the west coast of both North and South America (including Chile), the plates are mainly forcing themselves against each other – although in some sections they are touching but then also sliding in opposite directions (which is what was happening in Haiti); in some other areas, volcanoes erupt because of the thinning of the earth's crust. This is the world in which we live. (See diagram on page 54.)

We also need to note that the results of the 2004 tsunami were greatly increased by human action. Humans cleared areas of trees and other vegetation, and took away natural protection, all in order to provide beachside holiday accommodation for affluent tourists. Humans decided not to install the vital early warning system out in the ocean that could have saved so many lives (now partly installed and thus greatly reducing the deaths from the Indonesian tsunami of 2009). What about earthquakes? Geologist Professor Iain Stewart, in his TV series *How Earth Made Us* suggested that *earthquakes do not kill people; buildings do.* Crowded cities with poorly constructed buildings experience the most destruction. A large number of Haiti's buildings were not built as 'people-safe'. It was humans who used cheap materials to build a school in the Chinese earthquake zone, resulting in its collapse in the colossal Sichuan earthquake in 2008, and causing the deaths of most of its students. Not only that, but the engineers who in 2004 built the huge dam three miles from the epicentre of that earthquake now admit that it may have been seepage due to the weight of water in the dam that triggered the earthquake, which caused a total of 68,000 deaths. The effects of human action are also glaringly obvious when we consider global warming, which could eventually have devastating results throughout the world.

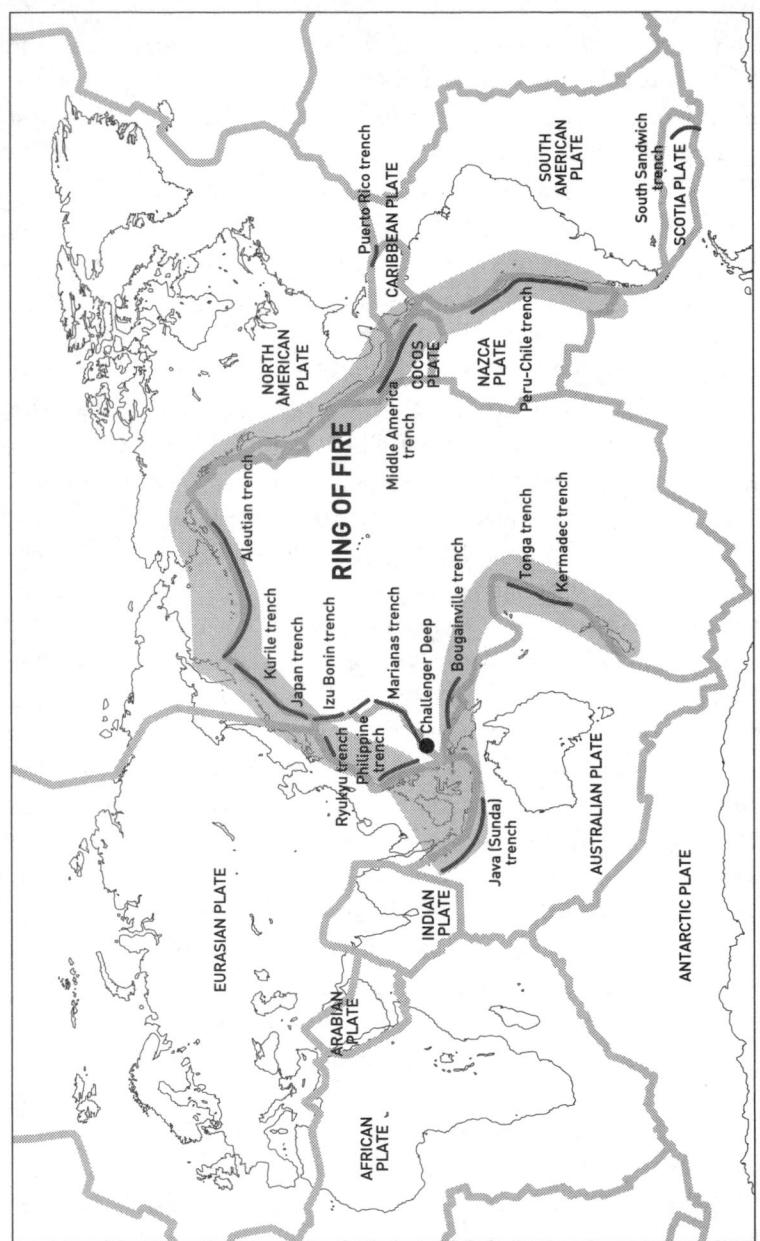

The main tectonic plates of the world and the Ring of Fire.

On the other hand, it is we humans who now have the intelligence to see the benefit from the fault lines who also now have the intelligence to build people-safe buildings, so that the infrastructure of cities can hopefully withstand the shocks and thus make human survival more possible (cities with people-safe buildings have few deaths in an earthquake). But it still takes the will and the wherewithal to build like that, so the task seems sadly unrealistic to poorer nations, unless the richer nations come in with substantial help.

*   *   *   *   *

We should surely be amazed that this world with its history of tumultuous and calamitous events, can support life at all. At the end of his superb 2010 BBC television series, *Wonders of the Solar System*, in which we saw the extraordinary seething worlds 'out there', Professor Brian Cox said that as this earth is driven by the same forces, 'I suppose it is a miracle that we exist at all'. Indeed it is!

One essential constituent for building the bodies of living creatures is carbon, yet no carbon came out of the 'Big Bang'. The amazing processes by which carbon was formed, such as the need to fuse together three helium nuclei almost *simultaneously* (which is almost impossible), and then how the carbon could be got out of a star at a temperature of millions of degrees, so stunned the British astrophysicist Fred Hoyle,[3] who discovered this carbon-producing process in the stars, that he moved from being the archetypal atheistic scientist to being one who spoke of 'Him who fixed it', the idea of a guiding hand leaving him 'greatly shaken'. For Christians, the 'Him', of course, is our Creator God and we praise Him for the amazing wonder of this universe, and for the incredible way we have been given the gift of life.

Those who insist life happened only by chance should hear the Astronomer Royal, Professor Sir Martin Rees, and the world-class mathematician Professor Sir Roger Penrose, who have both suggested that the likelihood of a universe giving us life coming into existence by coincidence is one in billions of billions, even one in trillions of trillions … or more.

Stephen Hawking writes in *A Brief History of Time*: 'It would be very difficult to explain why the universe should have begun in just such a way, except as the act of a God who intended to create human beings.'[4]

Physicist Freeman Dyson wrote: 'The more I examine the universe and the details of its architecture, the more evidence I find that the universe in some sense must have known we were coming.'[5]

When we think about the incredible way the world has been formed, and life given and sustained, it should not cause us to blame God, but rather to praise and thank Him with awed hearts that our life is possible in spite of (and also because of) the volcanic movements and eruptions and the influences of the rest of the universe. After the Haiti earthquake, our TV screens showed us young people there who were singing and praising God, not because of the destruction, but because of their living relationship with God which nothing could break.

Scientist Professor Robert White comments: 'One of the insights of geology for me is the amazing providence of God in creating a home just right for humans to inhabit.' He says that one of the most amazing facts about the earth is that it has maintained a temperature of between 0 and 100°C despite the sun getting 30 per cent hotter over the same period and the earth having slowed four- or five-fold: 'Without that consistency of surface temperature, life as we know it could not have survived.'[6] In Hebrews 1, we have our eyes lifted to the Son of God, 'through whom' God 'made the universe', but who is also 'sustaining all things by his powerful word' (vv.2–3, italics mine). Dr Denis Alexander writes: 'My own view reflects a robust expression of God's omnipotence that highlights God's faithfulness in both creating and *sustaining* the properties of matter, properties which, as a matter of fact, do perfectly fulfil his intentions and purposes' (italics mine).[7] What we have seen is that the movement of the tectonic plates is a vital part of that sustaining.

Yet, as Paul says in Romans 8:20, 'the creation was subjected to frustration'. He speaks of it being in 'bondage to decay' (v.21) and 'groaning' (v.22). What we call 'the cosmic Fall' is intertwined with the sin of humanity. The turning against God in Genesis 3 affected our relationship with God, and human relationships. It also affected the earth. Humans, being made in God's image, were told to act as God's stewards for all living things (Gen. 1:28), but sin has so often twisted that stewardship with self-interest that many have appallingly abused this responsibility for the world's resources and living beings.

In Romans 8, Paul lifts our eyes and hearts as he writes of the creation being subjected 'in hope' that it will be 'liberated from its bondage to decay and brought into the glorious freedom of the children of God' (vv.20–21) and, he says, we share with creation in 'eager expectation' (v.19). Of course, this does not release us from stewardship now, and we should be ashamed as Christians when we or fellow believers ignore and even abuse this stewardship. Thankfully, however, great numbers of believers are involved in the growing conservation movement and in seeking to offset, resist and even reverse the effects of human sin on this our (in reality, His) world. In doing so, we are being responsible stewards for God.

Eventually, says 2 Peter 3:12–13, the 'day of God' will come, which 'will bring about the destruction of the heavens by fire, and the elements will melt in the heat' but we are to be constantly encouraged because, 'in keeping with his promise we are looking forward to a new heaven and a new earth, the home of righteousness'. In the memorable words from Narnia, the term will be over and the holidays will have begun![8]

NOTES

1   The geological, oceanographic, meteorological, biological (both macro and micro)
    systems acting under the energy flux from the sun (which drives it all) and the
    cosmological appear to act as a closely coupled set of independent mechanisms to maintain
    the conditions for life. The movement of the tectonic plates is essential in this process.
    They, with the sun, renew and drive ocean currents, renew and enhance carbon
    dioxide absorbing bacteria from the depths of the ocean plate movements ... and so
    much more. (Dr C. Connolly; see Chapter 8, note 7.)

2   Dr Alister McGrath, Professor in Theology, Ministry and Education at King's College
    London. From his article 'Science, faith and making sense of things' in the book Real
    Scientists, Real Faith, ed. R.J. Berry (Oxford: Monarch Books, 2009).

3   Sir Fred Hoyle, FRS, 1915–2001, English astronomer.

4   Professor Stephen Hawking, A Brief History of Time (New York: Bantam Press, 1998),
    p.144. Stephen Hawking was Lucasian Professor of Mathematics at Cambridge
    University, 1979–2009.

5   Professor F. Dyson, cited in John D. Barrow, Frank J. Tipler, John A. Wheeler, The
    Anthropic Cosmological Principle, p.318; quoted by Francis Collins in his The Language of
    God (London: Simon & Schuster, 2007).

6   Professor Robert White, FRS, co-founder and Fellow of the Faraday Institute for Science
    and Religion at St Edmund's College, Cambridge, in his chapter 'Earthquakes, volcanoes
    and other catastrophes' in ed. R.J. Berry, Real Scientists, Real Faith (Oxford: Monarch
    Books, 2009). I also appreciate his further help to me.

7   Dr Denis Alexander, Creation or Evolution: Do We Have to Choose? (Oxford: Monarch
    Books, 2008), p.284. Dr Alexander is Director of the Faraday Institute for Science and
    Religion, St. Edmund's College, Cambridge. My thanks for his kind help.

8   From C.S. Lewis' The Last Battle, copyright © C.S. Lewis Pte. Limited, 1956. Adapted and
    reprinted by permission. Spoken by Aslan in the last chapter.

SEVEN

Why doesn't God stop all illness and disease?

'I'm not a religious person, but as soon as I got this serious illness, I prayed. I've still got the illness. Why doesn't God stop all illnesses and disease?'

'I'm a believing Christian and was led to believe that if I had enough faith (and no hidden sin), I could be healed of any illness or disease. I'm getting worse. Is it me at fault, or God?'

'If God is almighty, why did He not make humans in a better way, so that they never have illnesses?'

These cries come from the heart in the midst of an illness. How do we respond?

Firstly, we must be realistic about the way in which we are made. Carbon is vital for all life, and the way in which it was formed is mind-blowing. The principal elements in the human body are oxygen (65 per cent), then carbon (18 per cent), then hydrogen (10 per cent). That is how we are made. Carbon occurs throughout the whole body and is the vital ingredient that holds the elements together. Dr Denis Alexander explains: 'Life as we know it depends on the remarkable chemical combining power of carbon. Carbon is like one of those Lego bricks with knobbly bits on four of its sides that can be used to stick to other bits to make almost anything.'[1] Carbon-based life involves decay and death. We may think God should not have made us like that, but how else is life to be formed, as carbon is vital for all life? We are living organisms, our bodies changing all the time; we cannot be stainless steel robots who are decay-proof and death-proof.

Decay begins, we are told, soon after we are twenty years of age. The cosmetic industry certainly makes a profit out of gradual decay! There are many aids to our keeping fit these days, and plenty of warnings about the risks to health of drugs, drink, smoking and a bad diet. We can do a lot to fight bodily decay! We become much more conscious of 'decay' in our seventies and eighties, as the psalmist tells us 'The length of our days is seventy years – or eighty, if we have the strength' (Psa. 90:10). Shakespeare's 'All the world's a stage' speech from *As You Like It* dramatises it, ending with that unforgettable phrase 'sans teeth, sans eyes, sans taste, sans everything'![2] Henry Francis Lyte (1793–1847) gave it a more uplifting dimension in the hymn 'Abide With Me': 'Change and decay in all around I see; O Lord, who changes not, abide with me.'

Pain is what causes suffering, and none of us wants it. However, go to people suffering from leprosy, who have lost all sense of pain, and we realise how necessary pain is as a warning system that something is wrong, and how dangerous it is when we don't feel any pain (for example, burning our hands on a hot pan). So it is possible to see pain as part of God's gracious gift to us, although, while that attitude helps our spirit, it does not relieve the pain![3]

Pain is always difficult to bear, but especially so when it has gone on for years. A lady tackled me recently when she heard I was writing on suffering. 'What do you know about suffering?' she said. 'I have had pain for twenty years.' She had my sympathy, not least because I *have* known some suffering, but mine has been short-lived, like that of most people. To have it for twenty years must be very difficult to bear. We all want to do everything we can to reduce pain, or alleviate it. Our Lord's concern is shown, for instance, in Matthew 4:24: '… people brought to him all who were ill with various diseases, those suffering severe pain …'

Edith Schaeffer wrote: 'Affliction must be recognised as something we all need to deal with. There is no place to go for a vacation from the abnormality of the universe, from the effects of the Fall upon every area of life, and from the conflict of the ages. Persecution and affliction are a *normal* part of the Christian life.'[4] If we accept that how we are made is the only way that human life can exist, our attitude changes. We can move from the 'Why?' to the 'How?' – which is what the next section of this book is all about.

Secondly, we need to understand why some people sadly get a birth disability or a serious illness. Something is going wrong with their bodies. Dr Alexander helps us over this, too: 'without genetic variation between us all, we would all be clonal, looking identical. But it is the same genetic variation which affects our susceptibility to certain diseases, and which causes genetic diseases or cancers – necessary costs of living in a carbon-based world.'[5] Similarly, the scientist–theologian Dr John Polkinghorne says that exactly the same biochemical processes that allow cells to mutate and produce new forms of life will allow other cells to mutate and become malignant, and he goes on to say that, for instance, the presence of cancer is 'neither a gratuitous horror nor the product of creatoral incompetence'.[6]

We might add that, except for when we have caused the illness ourselves, we are talking about randomness in how these physical things hit one and not another. This removes in a stroke any query such as, 'Why has God let this happen to me?' or 'What have I done to deserve this?' I am asked: 'What about Psalm 31:15: "My times are in your hands"?' We have to see the whole psalm to understand that phrase. The psalmist describes his sufferings, his eyes wasting away from grief, his soul and body also. His strength fails, his bones waste away. His adversaries scorn him. This is how life has hit him, but he does not blame God nor think his times are not in God's hands … he trusts God's steadfast love. Those hands of love hold him and undergird his life. His times are very securely in God's hands.

Thirdly, it has been a help to me to be shown something of the incredible complexity of the human body, as Dr Colin Connolly has helpfully shown:[7]

• **Each human body has more cells in it than there are stars in the universe;**
• **Each one is about 0.01 mm across;**
• **Each cell contains about 2,000 mitochondria which are responsible for making energy at constant temperature for use in the body;**

- Each mitochondrion depends on hundreds of chemical reactions facilitating electron transfer and if one system fails then disease or disorder results (emphasis mine);
- The human brain has about 100 billion nerve cells;
- Each cell is linked to 25,000–100,000 others;
- Synapses between cells constantly form and dissolve, weaken and strengthen in response to new experiences and learning;
- The synapses are awash with hormones which modulate responses;
- Many specific neurotransmitters in the synapses are made by DNA encoding programs which modulate nerve transmission;
- Soft logic is normal – on, off and 'maybe';
- Processing capacity is estimated at 2.5 million gigabytes.

When I read this, and I am told that it would take a huge room to house a computer, using today's technology, to achieve the same gigabyte capacity as the human brain, I do not ask why our bodies go wrong, but rather marvel at how our amazingly complex living bodies are made and that they 'work' wonderfully most of the time. With the psalmist, my heart cries, 'I praise you because I am fearfully and wonderfully made' (Psa. 139:14).

Fourthly, we are now into a thrilling new era of gene discovery, giving the hope of tackling all sorts of illnesses that have been incurable up to now. In this, we can see that, although God could only make us as carbon-based, He has also provided within our incredible bodies the ways to tackle the illnesses and diseases. Professor John Wyatt writes: 'In the search for new and effective medical therapies, the Christian understanding of creation supports the idea of a remarkable healing potential locked within the human body.'[8]

The human genome, consisting of all the DNA species, is the hereditary code of life. It is, we are told, 3 billion letters long! The leader of the International Human Genome Project, 'which had laboured mightily over more than a decade to reveal the DNA Sequence', is Dr Francis S. Collins, who is also a committed Christian. He writes of how, soon after the millennium began, 'the amazing script, carrying within it all of the instructions for building a human being, was available to the world'.[9] It was a day of momentous significance for the whole world. With links to other world leaders by satellite, President Clinton said, 'Without a doubt, this is the most important, most wondrous map ever produced by mankind' and, further on in his speech, 'Today we are learning the language in which God created life. We are gaining ever more awe for the complexity, the beauty, and the wonder of God's most divine and sacred gift.'

I was not surprised to hear recently that a first-year medical student was so amazed by the intricacy and beauty of DNA that she started to seek God for the first time (and found Him!). Now we are used to hearing frequently about the discerning of particular genes as the root of this or that disease or illness. The future medically is exciting, thanks to the way we are made by our amazing God!

Of course, as believers, we have to be on our guard, as even these wonderful discoveries can be abused, as exemplified by the attempts to search for 'transhumanism'.[10]

We are also being challenged by the lobbying for assisted suicide and euthanasia. Michael Wenham in his book *My Donkey Body* writes movingly against it, and he has the right to speak from his MND perspective. Professor John Wyatt has major chapters on it in his great book *Matters of Life and Death* (see note 8).

There is no doubting that we would all prefer perfect health, and for diseases to be removed from the world, but that is the 'not yet' world, not the 'now' world. Romans 8 declares that we humans are part of the creation 'subjected to frustration' (v.20), but equally, we are part of the creation that 'will be liberated from its bondage to decay' (v.21). That we can turn suffering to become a testimony to God's grace and glory will be the uplifting theme of the next section of the book, but we finish this section by lifting our eyes to the time of new and transformed bodies:

Philippians 3:20–21   'But our citizenship is in heaven. And we eagerly await a Saviour from there, the Lord Jesus Christ, who, by the power that enables him to bring everything under his control, will transform our lowly bodies so that they will be like his glorious body.'

1 Corinthians 15:42–44 'So will it be with the resurrection of the dead. The body that is sown is perishable, it is raised imperishable; it is sown in dishonour, it is raised in glory; it is sown in weakness, it is raised in power; it is sown a natural body, it is raised a spiritual body.'

Or to put it another way, our new resurrection bodies will be even more amazing!

NOTES

1   Dr Denis Alexander, *Creation or Evolution: Do We Have to Choose?* (Oxford: Monarch Books, 2008), pp.336–337.
2   William Shakespeare, *As You Like It*. Last line of Jaques' speech: 'All the world's a stage ...'
3   A very helpful book, which opens up the relation of leprosy and pain is *The Gift of Pain* by Philip Yancey and Paul Brand – subtitled *Why We Hurt and What We Can Do About It* (Grand Rapids, MI: Zondervan, 1997).
4   Edith Schaeffer, *Affliction* (London: Hodder & Stoughton, 1984), p.28.
5   Dr Denis Alexander, *Creation or Evolution*: op.cit. p.280.
6   Dr John Polkinghorne, *Scientists as Theologians* (London: SPCK, 1996), pp.45–46.
7   I am grateful to Dr Colin Connolly, DSc PhD MS BSc ARCS, for writing this piece for the book. He was formerly Chief Scientist at the DoH and a senior World Health Organisation Consultant. My thanks to him for his help.
8   Professor John Wyatt, whose help I appreciate, is Professor of Ethics and Perinatology at University College Hospital London, and Honorary Consultant Neonatologist at University College London Hospital. Chapter entitled 'No easy answers' in ed. R.J Berry *Real Scientists, Real Faith*. See also his brilliant book *Matters of Life and Death* (Revised edition Leicester: IVP, 2009), which includes chapters on assisted suicide and euthanasia.
9   Dr Francis S. Collins, *The Language of God*. Dr Collins is one of the USA's leading geneticists. This book gives details about the amazing complexity and beauty of DNA. (These can be read and seen on the Internet eg Wikipedia.) I am grateful for his warm support.
10 Dr Denis Alexander, 'Enhancing Humans or a New Creation?' (*Cambridge Papers*, Vol. 18, No. 2, June 2009, The Jubilee Centre, 3 Hooper St, Cambridge CB1 2NZ). He says that 'transhumanism' has gained a significant foothold in academic life. It is the idea that ageing is an illness that can be overcome by enhancement technologies 'giving abilities integral to the body beyond those we would normally consider a human to possess'. Dr Alexander shows the falsity of this concept and says: 'it is not transhumans or posthumans we need in society, but more transformed humans.'

SECTION B
HOW?
KNOWING THE GOD OF LOVE

EIGHT

The transforming relationship with the God of love

When I was sixteen, I was given a ticket for an afternoon performance of Haydn's *Creation* at the Royal Albert Hall. It was for a box in a prime position. That day there was smog in London and it had seeped into the Hall, giving an ethereal feel. There was a large orchestra, a huge choir and the great organ. I was taken totally by surprise when it came to 'And God said ... Let there be light ... And there was ... *Light!*' Every instrument, every voice and, it seemed, every part of the organ, gave the fullest force to that word. The contrast was huge. I actually fell backwards in the chair I was sitting on. What an impact! What a way of expressing the power of God!

Yet, in 2 Corinthians 4:6, we read these amazing words: 'For God, who said, "Let light shine out of darkness," made his light shine in our hearts to give us the light of the knowledge of the glory of God in the face of Christ.' The God of the universe has shone in our hearts! – in OUR hearts! It is staggering; it is wonderful; it is true in our experience. I do not fall off my chair in shock and amazement as I did in the Royal Albert Hall, but rather fall to my knees in wonder and awe.

What happens to those who turn to Christ and are born anew by the Spirit is not just illumination of divine truth (although that certainly does happen), but the knowledge of God 'in the face of Christ'. This is personalised into a relationship with our Saviour and Lord.

I hate religion or, at least, the word 'religion'. It speaks of rules and laws, and doing this and not doing that. But Christianity is Christ. Christianity is coming into relationship with God in Christ. It is the relationship God intended for all humans, but it was broken by our

67

ancestors in the Fall. So it is not a new relationship that we receive through Christ, but a restored relationship which sin had broken. Christianity is not first about rules; it is about knowing God as Father, and Christ as our Saviour, Lord and Friend. It is being able to talk with Him and slip our hand into His hand as we walk through life. It is about pouring our heart out to Him and burying our head in His chest without any words. It is knowing He is with us in the valley of the shadow of death (Psa. 23), in 'a den of lions' (Dan. 6), or even in martyrdom (Stephen in Acts 7:55). We never walk alone!

So important is the deepening of this relationship before or during suffering that before Paul expounds on suffering in Romans 8 (from v.18), he takes the first seventeen verses to deepen our understanding of the relationship we have with God in Christ. Paul knows this is vital to grasp if we are to face the challenges he sets out in the second half of the chapter. Chapters 1–7 of Romans have shown how we can get right with God through Christ's death for our sins on the cross, and how the new relationship begins. Now in chapter 8 he underlines the assurance of 'no condemnation', of being set free from the law of sin and death by the Spirit, of our minds influenced by the Spirit, the assurance of our resurrection, of our being God's children, of knowing God as Father. So the believer is in a completely different dimension of life from the unbeliever when facing suffering, or 'sharing in Christ's sufferings' (see v.17), because of this wonderful relationship with God in Christ into which we have been brought.

'Just a minute!' said a Christian counsellor, when I spoke to her about this. 'There are many people in the church who cannot understand what is meant by relationship; they have been hurt, abused, without any relationship that was meaningful in their childhood and youth. They have suffered lovelessness, so they cannot grasp what it means to have a spiritual love-relationship with Christ. Their experience of fatherhood also makes the concept of God as a loving Father difficult to accept.'

Difficult, but not impossible. Good Christian counselling can help bring gradual healing, sometimes over a period of years. An emotionally wounded person can also begin to find a relationship with God through the security of being loved and cared for by other Christians.

Millions have woken up to this relationship through the exposition of Scripture and, like John Wesley, found their heart 'strangely warmed'. For me, it was through getting on my knees and telling Him I longed to know Him in fuller reality. I have known some to have found it as a result of receiving bereavement ministry. One bereaved lady I know who received such ministry testified that after fifty-six years in the church, only now could she say she knew God.

I am saddened when people tell me that they 'try to be a good Christian', but say that they lack the 'glow' or 'what others seem to have'. If anyone reading this knows that this is your need, may I encourage you to contact a person you know who has this genuine warmth of a relationship with Christ, and meet with them to help you find it for yourself.

There are still others who have taken this step and have begun that relationship, yet are still unsure. Romans 8 explains that it is as the Spirit influences our minds that we are gradually able to make this truth our own. Therefore, the uncertain person needs to come to the New Testament with a longing heart, and pray that the Spirit will make the Word of God come alive, and the reality of relationship with Christ more real. A wise Christian minister, counsellor or friend may be able to help with this.

Sometimes, as Romans 8:12–13 expounds, we may be leading a double life and not dealing with the things that belong to our sinful nature, and again need to take action, however costly. We will never know the reality of relationship with God when known sin is blocking it. Nor will we if we are unable to forgive others.

As the truth and experience deepen, we can truly set aside fear, cry from the heart 'Abba, Father' (Rom. 8:15) and know, through the deeper experience of the Spirit witnessing with our spirit, that we are God's children (Rom. 8:16). It is then that we are more able to walk through suffering with our Lord.

All relationships have to grow in trust, in understanding, in harmony and in love. When I said 'I love you' to my wife, Myrtle, on our wedding day in 1956, I meant it from the heart. But fifty-four years on, it is infinitely fuller in its meaning through the deepening effect of the multifaceted experiences of life, including suffering. So it is in our relationship with Christ. Rather than troubles bringing us to doubt this relationship, they should be the catalyst for deepening it. We are thrown more upon Him. We come closer to Him. We are experiencing more of having that treasure in our jars of clay (2 Cor. 4:7)! We are learning more about what it is to abide in Him, and He in us (John 15:4). We can trust Him even when we do not understand the 'why?' of our suffering.

NINE

Strengthening faith in God as God

Now faith is being sure of what we hope for and certain of what we do not see ... without faith it is impossible to please God ... (Hebrews 11:1,6)

The three main pillars of the Christian life are faith, love and hope, and they need to become stronger and stronger. They stand on the rock of Christ and are strengthened by the Holy Spirit.

So first we look at the pillar of faith.

Suffering puts faith to the test. When we are physically vulnerable, it is a place where doubt can come, and where we are open to spiritual attack. We see this in the life of our Lord, when He is tempted by the devil for forty days and forty nights in the Judean wilderness. The devil plays on the suffering of physical hunger and tries to push our Lord into misusing His divine powers for His own need: 'If you are the Son of God, tell these stones to become bread' (Matt. 4:3). In this and the other temptations, the devil is trying to deflect Christ from His mission. This also seems to be Paul's meaning when in 2 Corinthians 12:7 he describes his 'thorn in the flesh' as 'a messenger of Satan, to • torment me'. Christ met His temptation with the Word of God, and Paul meets it with fresh resolve in the grace and power of Christ.

Satan figures prominently in the vivid drama of the book of Job.[1] The picture given us of sufferings piling up one after the other leaves us breathless. Satan thinks Job's faith will be smashed by suffering. Job feels desolate, abandoned and powerless, but his faith survives – just – and eventually it becomes transformed by being shown the extent of God's power and majesty. He is overwhelmed in worship. His life is restored.

It is in the context of suffering for the faith that in 1 Peter 5:8–9 we are bidden to 'Be self-controlled and alert. Your enemy the devil prowls around like a roaring lion looking for someone to devour. Resist him, standing firm in the faith, because you know that your brothers throughout the world are undergoing the same kind of sufferings.'

In Paul's description in Ephesians 6:10–18, of the full armour of God that we need to put on in our struggle 'against the authorities, against the powers of this dark world and against the spiritual forces of evil in the heavenly realms' (v.12), it is the 'shield of faith' with which we can 'extinguish all the flaming arrows of the evil one' (v.16). When we are weak, we are vulnerable to spiritual attack.

Paul is so concerned for the Thessalonian church in the sufferings hitting them, that as 'Satan stopped' him (1 Thess. 2:18), he sent Timothy. The purpose? 'To strengthen and encourage you in your faith, so that no-one would be unsettled by these trials' (1 Thess. 3:2–3). Later, Paul could praise them because of their 'perseverance and faith in all the persecutions and trials' they were enduring, and because their faith was 'growing more and more' rather than withering (2 Thess. 1:3–4). So we see how important the strengthening of faith is in the experiences of suffering.

*   *   *   *   *

How deeply is our faith anchored in God? Can it withstand attacks and not be destroyed? How does such faith take deeper root within us? What can prevent it from doing so?

'Just trust that the water will hold you up,' they said. Perhaps because I did not really trust, I did not succeed in letting my body lie flat. Without real trust, I could not float. I had not learnt to swim as a child, as the army had commandeered our town's swimming pool. Trust was more difficult as an adult. An experience in childhood had also damaged my confidence. I had fallen off the sea wall into deep water. My father and brother dived in to pull me out. I was very frightened and I cried with shock for a long time. So perhaps my trust was damaged then.

For some people, the faith that can trust God whatever happens to them in life is difficult to make their own. This may be because they received wrong ideas in childhood, claiming that all we have to do is pray and God will give us what we want. For example, a child prays for a relative not to die. They die. Faith is harmed or shattered. With some people, it may be that they have never been able to trust anyone, let alone God. Then there are those adults who will only attend their local church's family service. They believe, but unless they get into adult thinking and hear adult teaching about the faith, their faith is always going to be at child level. If tragedy strikes, they are finished. They do not go to church again. As Edith Schaeffer wrote, 'we are too easily turned toward thinking of what we can "get" in the way of happiness by being a Christian'.[2]

I did eventually learn to swim. Trust came. Progress through the water was now possible. Practice made my swimming stronger. Faith had now produced action. I could swim to an offshore rock. I could handle troubled water.

The first steps of faith are much easier for some than for others. For some, it is progress when they can say, like the father in Mark 9:24, 'I do believe; help me overcome my unbelief!' Faith does not have to wait for all questions to be answered. Some answers will only be grasped once we *have* faith. When the heart begins to open up to God, faith is then pointed to Jesus. We come to see and trust that He is the Son of God, and that He came into this world to die for our sins and to bring us into His eternal family. John 3:16 states that '... God so loved the world that he gave his one and only Son, that whoever *believes* in him shall not perish but have eternal life.' In Romans 5:1, Paul says that we are 'justified through *faith*', and in Ephesians 2:8, 'by grace you have been saved, through *faith*' (all italics mine).

But if faith stops there, it is not ready for suffering. It is a faith that brings us assurance of salvation, but we must move into a faith that trusts God to help us do His will, to be His servants and witnesses, to live for His glory. It is a faith that grows through experience. Just as a diver learns to dive from the lower, then the middle, and finally the top board, God will help us to grow in faith. We see it with Abraham

(Gen. 12 onwards) as he first leaves home at God's command, travels into unknown territory, faces famine, has to rescue Lot, and is given the great promises of God as an everlasting covenant. Then he comes to the 'top board' lesson with his only son, Isaac, and the readiness to sacrifice him if that is what God wants (Gen. 22:1–19). Faith was not just in words or in a creed. It was proved by action, as James 2:14–24 sharply teaches.

Clear-cut responses to our faith and to our prayers will encourage us to see that God knows our situation, but the next stage is learning to trust Him even when we see no obvious response. In the terrific end to Romans 8, we see faith holding to the truth that nothing can separate us from the love of Christ, and Paul quotes, 'For your sake we face death all day long; we are considered as sheep to be slaughtered' (v.36). Yet faith holds.

This same deeply embedded faith is seen in Habakkuk, with respect to disasters in the world – floods, plagues, earthquakes. His heart pounds, his lips quiver, decay creeps into his bones, his legs tremble. Yet in Habakkuk 3:17–19 he says,

> **Though the fig-tree does not bud and there are no grapes on the vines, though the olive crop fails and the fields produce no food, though there are no sheep in the pen and no cattle in the stalls, yet I will rejoice in the Lord, I will be joyful in God my Saviour. The Sovereign Lord is my strength.**

Instead of losing faith, he worships with joy!

We see that faith in David when his child dies (2 Sam. 12:15–23). For seven days he had fasted and pleaded with God for the child. Now, when he is told that the child is dead, his reaction is to wash, change his clothes and to go into the house of the Lord to worship. Only then did he eat. How many of us, as Christians, would first go and worship? This is trust in action.

C.S. Lewis had written so brilliantly about the problem of pain, yet even he was devastated when his beloved wife, Joy, died. He felt God had shut and bolted the door. Emotion overtook him like a flood. He eventually emerged from his darkness of despair and sorrow, and tells us about it in *A Grief Observed*, but in the book he pulls no punches about the battering that faith can receive.

David Watson[3] had a very fruitful and effective ministry, with special gifts of evangelism. He was known throughout the Christian world. When he was diagnosed with terminal cancer, the shock to him and his wife, Anne (and to the Christian world), was colossal. Their first prayer was, 'Heavenly Father, we know you love us and are fully in control of our lives. Help us to trust you, and keep us in your peace. We really need your help. Amen.' Asking God to help them to trust Him, that was the key. But David's faith was 'ferociously attacked'. In the middle of the night, with the body at its lowest, he found that although he had preached all over the world without doubting the truths in Christ, he was now plagued by doubt, waking up in a cold sweat. He recalled the words of Dostoevsky: 'It is not as a child that I believe and confess Jesus Christ. My "hosanna" is born of a furnace of doubt.'

David Watson's doubts and questionings did not last for long. He ended his account of that battle with these words: 'I am not saying that I never had any problems after that. It would not be true. But in the middle of those nightmare storms, with the waves of doubt and fear lashing all around me, I found that my faith was secure on that immovable rock of Christ.' Later on, he found that his faith could remain positive as he went on thanking God for the truth of His Word, and the power of the Spirit within him.

When God lists his 'Honours Board' in Hebrews 11, everyone on it is there because of their faith. It is not just a saving faith but *a faith in God as God*. The list is filled with the names of those who put faith into action – Noah, Abraham, Moses, Gideon and their like – where the outcome was great. We cheer. But then we read of the faith that stands even in what the world would call 'defeat'. From verse 35 we read of those who were tortured, who '... faced jeers and flogging, while still others were chained and put in prison. They were stoned; they were sawn in two; they were put to death by the sword. They went about in sheepskins and goatskins, destitute, persecuted and ill-treated'. These are all commended for their *faith*. That is faith at the highest level, that stands the greatest test. It is the faith of the martyrs through the centuries, their tremendous courage in being thrown to the lions, or burnt at the stake, or hacked to death by cannibals. Such courage could only have been possible because of a deeply rooted faith.

We cannot begin to imagine the horror and suffering of all these saints of old, such pain and such agony, yet they still held on to their faith. In our own day, we shudder at how Christians are being mercilessly persecuted in several parts of the world.

For other believers, the suffering is more personal, but is no less real. Michael Wenham, writing movingly of his struggle with motor neurone disease,[4] says that faith is not a 'panacea for pain'. To meet his own situation, Michael Mayne,[5] dying of cancer, found it helpful to repeat with fervour the words from Philippians 4:13: 'I can do all things through [Christ] who strengthens me' (NRSV). As he became weaker and dependent on others, he wrote, 'Trapped by time, daily a little nearer death, yet having eternity with me in the day that is called today because I have faith that I am (in Christ) in a relationship with One whom I daily call "Abba, Father".' In the depths of such suffering, faith needs maintaining, if possible, on a daily basis, but that will spring from a faith that has been deeply worked through and established in our very being.

So, my plea to myself and to fellow believers is to work at deepening faith when we are fit and well, even to welcome 'minor' tests of faith as being ways of strengthening us, so that we are not overwhelmed if greater suffering comes to us. Doubts will attack. Satan knows that if he can break our faith, he has separated us from the One who alone can carry us through. So, perhaps we need to keep Ephesians 6:16 always in front of us: '... take up the shield of faith, with which you can extinguish all the flaming arrows of the evil one.' Taking it up daily when all is well will help us to make it a normal part of our life even when we are suffering.

It is appropriate at this stage to recall Bob Mortimer's honesty about faith in the midst of his suffering (see Chapter 2): 'There have been plenty of times when my faith has faltered, when I have become overwhelmed with the depressing nature of my immediate circumstances ... but the Lord has always been there for me. I have learnt to have a greater trust and dependence on God. I could not cope with this situation without his help and strength.' It reminds us again of Psalm 63:8: 'My soul clings to you; your right hand upholds me.'

Michael Wenham in *My Donkey Body* tells of the time when he fell out of bed in the night and his means of communication with his wife was out of reach. He was helpless; he needed to relieve himself; he was alone. So graphic is his description that I hardly slept the night after reading it, feeling for him. He must have felt that he was clinging to God by his fingertips. I have had several operations in the course of my life but after one, for an abscessed appendix, I was so affected, presumably by the morphine and by the poison that had leaked for days from the abscess, that I did not know what to do with my body ... no position relieved it. I even dismissed the chaplain who brought me Holy Communion as I could not cope with anything except a brief prayer. It was a case of 'physician, heal yourself' as I sought to practise what I had preached, which was to hold on to God. I took one thought about Him and held on to it hour after hour; the next day, another thought. On the third day, the physical state eased and I felt wrapped around by a blanket of love – God's love. Faith had helped me to cling on to God, and God's right hand had upheld me. It was tough while it lasted. Yet this was only for two days. To endure this day after day after day must be so draining and must test faith to the limit.

There can be no more helpful place to go to, as we face suffering, than the garden of Gethsemane. We can never know the depth of the suffering our Lord faced: the physical pain – from the terrible, lacerating flogging and the excruciating torture of the crucifixion; pain as a human being like us but, far more, the pain of feeling separate from His Father, the pain of bearing the sins of the world. Yet His faith in His Father did not fail, for it was deep within His very being, and He knew that nothing could separate Him (nor us, as believers) from the Father. On the cross, He confidently promises paradise to the thief alongside Him, cries, 'It is finished' and prays, 'Father, into your hands I commit my spirit' (Luke 23:43; John 19:30; Luke 23:46). His faith is strong to the end.

Let us be those who pray: 'Lord, help me have such a faith, to the end, whatever lies ahead in my life.'

NOTES

1 Chapter 9 of D.A. Carson's book *How Long, O Lord?* (Leicester: IVP, 1982) gives a very helpful study of Job.

2 Edith Schaeffer, *Affliction* (London: Hodder & Stoughton, 1984), p.29. Edith Schaeffer was the co-founder, with her husband Francis Schaeffer, of L'Abri Fellowship in Switzerland.

3 David Watson, *Fear No Evil* (London: Hodder & Stoughton, 1984), pp.15,43,45,155. David Watson was vicar of St Michael-le-Belfry in York, and a worldwide evangelist.

4 Michael Wenham, *My Donkey Body* (Oxford: Monarch, 2008). He was vicar of Stanford in the Vale from 1989. I appreciate his warm readiness to let me quote several times from his moving book.

5 Michael Mayne, *The Enduring Melody* (London: Darton Longman and Todd, 2006), pp.60,198. Michael Mayne was Head of Religious Programmes, BBC Radio, vicar of Great St Mary's (the University Church), Cambridge and Dean of Westminster.

Deepening in assurance of the love of God

And now these three remain: faith, hope and love. But the greatest of these is love. (1 Corinthians 13:13)

'All You Need Is Love' is the title of the popular Beatles song. For anyone handling suffering, there is a real sense in which that is true. We all need to be loved, to know we are loved, and to go on loving others. The Christian has a far bigger dimension of love: we know that the love we 'need' most of all is God's love; we need to know that His love for us is sure, certain, unbreakable and everlasting ... that nothing can separate us from it. Even when we cannot feel that love we need to know that it remains, always.

The well-known poem by Mary Stevenson, 'Footprints in the Sand', which has been a comfort to very many people, expresses this well. The Christian and the Lord walk together across the sands of life, but in times of trouble the two sets of footprints become one. This dismays the Christian, who wrongly reads this as meaning the Lord has gone away; however, the one set of footprints is because the Lord was carrying him or her in His arms. This reminded my wife Myrtle of the time when our young daughter was rushed into hospital by ambulance with suspected meningitis, her little body so weak, so limp. There was nothing we could do for her physically. We felt helpless. But we were not helpless spiritually. We *could* entrust her into the arms of the Lord to carry her (and us) through whatever lay ahead – and He did.

Almost all the books, testimonies and articles by Christians going through suffering zoom in on God's love. For Michael Mayne,[1] this is the meaning of the title of his book, *The Enduring Melody*. Through the pilgrimage of his suffering, God's love is like a *cantus firmus*, a pattern of music that began with the Gregorian chants from the sixth century. Baroque composers like J.S. Bach used chorale music as the basic melody. Michael's point was that a *cantus firmus* is the one tune always present but is built on, elaborated, decorated, turned upside down. Through all the ups and downs of his suffering, first from ME and then terminal cancer, the *cantus firmus* of God's love never ceased for him. It is a beautiful way of seeing God's love.

When I was a choirboy, we chanted a different psalm each Sunday. When we came to Psalm 136, it seemed endless. Every one of its twenty-six verses has the refrain 'His love endures for ever'. I was a long way into my Christian life before the deep significance of this repetition began to grab my soul. A growing understanding of God's covenant love opened up my mind; it put God's love at the centre.[2] Here in this psalm was the belief that whatever happened in the world, in history or in daily life, one thing never changed – the love of God. When the people of Israel celebrated bringing the ark of the covenant to the Temple, for example, there was a multitude of musicians and a wide range of musical instruments, but only one song, 'He is good; his love endures for ever' (2 Chron. 5:12–13). On the other hand, several psalms – 106, 118 – speak of going through trouble or difficulty, yet still have 'Give thanks to the LORD, for he is good; his love endures for ever' as their anchor verse.

It is significant that the confidence of Psalm 136 is followed by the very downbeat mood of Psalm 137, written when the people of God were in exile in Babylon, and which speaks of not being able even to sing the Lord's song in a foreign land, their musical instruments falling silent and hanging on trees. There is no mention of God's love enduring for ever. Everything seemed to have been swept away, including their empty worship and disobedient actions. However, the prophets held on to the fact that God's love could not be swept away. The prophet Jeremiah was caught up in the Exile and in his book, Lamentations, does nothing to cheer the heart in its blackness until, suddenly, like a huge pyrotechnic display bursting into the dark sky, we read: 'Because of the LORD's great love we are not consumed, for his compassions never fail. They are new every morning; great is your faithfulness' (Lam. 3:22–23).

We love to sing the hymn 'Great is Thy faithfulness', but notice the words that follow in Lamentations 3:24: 'The Lord is my portion', showing a deep trust relationship that leads on to 'I will wait for him'. The people might have earlier celebrated with the song that God's love endures for ever, but it does not seem to have become part of their core belief. Only the prophets had meditated on it and now stood on the rock of that truth. For us, as New Testament Christians, there is a fundamental lesson here. We sing so frequently about God's love, especially with regard to the cross, but how deeply has it become part of our sure belief, ready to withstand the downs of life as well as the ups?

We are all so easily influenced by circumstances. In the disputes about global warming, it is far easier to believe in it when in the burning heat of 40°C in an area not used to such an extreme. It is not so easy to believe in it when enduring the coldest winter for one hundred years! Similarly, we can easily sing and speak of the love of God when all is well, but unless that belief is deep down in us, we will find it hard to sing of it or trust it when suffering.

Frances Young,[3] who faced this as she brought up her severely disabled son, wrote 'The tragedy was not so much Arthur as my sense of abandonment, my inability to accept the existence and love of God *at those deeper levels where it makes a real difference to one's life*' (italics mine).

Henry Venn, a great Christian of some 200 years ago, who was suddenly left with five young children when his wife died, wrote:

> **Did I not know the Lord to be mine, were I not certain his love feels even more love for me than I am able to conceive, were this not evident to me, not by deduction and argument, but by consciousness, by his own light shining in my soul as the sun does upon my bodily eyes, into what a deplorable condition should I have now been cast.**

During the time we were ministering in Manchester, 'Rose', a member of the Salvation Army, used to come to share with us because she loved the Holy Communion service. Her life had been largely trouble free. She was a lovely person. Then she became ill and was taken into hospital. Suddenly she doubted the love of God. Her roots in God's love were not as deep as she or we had presumed. My colleague Mary Hollinshead found this out on her visits to Rose. She said to her on one occasion, 'I am going to sit here for as long as it takes until you can say again from the heart that God is love. I will be praying and reading scriptures and sitting quietly.' I could not imagine myself doing that, but Mary was right. She knew that the roots just needed strengthening. Eventually Rose came to the point of regaining her belief in God's love and, when she returned to church, she stood up to tell us of her deepest gratitude to Mary, and her deep shock that she could ever have doubted God's love.

*   *   *   *   *

How then we do establish the enduring melody of God's love more deeply within us?

First and foremost it is by prayer. The main prayers of the New Testament are that God will produce spiritual growth in other Christians as well as in ourselves.

The major prayer about love is to be found in Ephesians 3:14–19:

> *I kneel before the Father, from whom his whole family in heaven and on earth derives its name. I pray that out of his glorious riches he may strengthen you with power through his Spirit in your inner being, so that Christ may dwell in your hearts through faith. And I pray that you, being rooted and established in love, may have power, together with all the saints, to grasp how wide and long and high and deep is the love of Christ, and to know this love that surpasses knowledge – that you may be filled to the measure of the fulness of God.*

If we look at it closely, we will see that Paul is so passionate about it that he kneels before the Father. The members of his churches are on his heart. He is obviously praying this sort of prayer for them very frequently. If he were pastoring a church today, this would be part of his daily prayer and he would encourage all members to pray this for one another and themselves (and the results would be dynamic). I did not wake up to this until late on in my ministry, and kicked myself for taking so long to realise how vital it is to pray in this way. It is fired by the heartache for every believer that they should have a fuller and fuller grasp and experience of God's love.

At the beginning of his prayer for the Ephesians, Paul prays for their strengthening through the Spirit within them, and we know from Romans 5:5 that this is God's side of helping us grow ('God has poured out his love into our hearts by the Holy Spirit'). He then prays that 'Christ may dwell in your hearts through faith'. The more we know Christ, the more we see love. Of course, most of all, we see God's love in the cross. But we hear our Lord say, 'As the Father has loved me, so have I loved you. Now remain in my love' (John 15:9). The closer our walk with Jesus, the more we know God's love.

In Ephesians 3:17, Paul's prayer comes to its kernel: 'I pray that you, being rooted and established in love …' And that is it! Our love should be so deep that illness, bereavement, disappointment, persecution, wars, crime, evil or any form of suffering cannot quench it. What a prayer for ourselves and for others! Paul then becomes more specific. He prays in Ephesians 3:18 that they will '… grasp how wide and long and high and deep is the love of Christ'. What a prayer! We will never plumb its depths or reach its heights. We may never fully see its width or length, but the prayer is for us to have our narrow vision blown open in every direction. Year after year we should be grasping more of the dimensions of that love, so much so that we come to the point of not just knowing more about this love, but getting to where it 'surpasses knowledge' (v.19). Because God is love, it follows that the consequence of this praying is 'that you may be filled … [with] all the fulness of God'. The most lovely and godly elderly Christians we know have deepened in that love over many years and through many experiences, not least through suffering. They glow with God's love.

So important is this prayer that I would want to encourage *every*

Christian reader (and I am saying this to myself as well) to reinforce such praying as part of their life and of their ministry to themselves and to others.

John Benson[4] was a clergyman in Singapore for twenty years until increasing weakness and fatigue led to his early retirement. He has been diagnosed with Charcot-Marie-Tooth disease, an illness which leads to the breakdown of nerve fibres and wasting of muscles in the arms and legs.

I asked him how he could still believe in God's love. He told me that he had gone to university as a shy and insecure student, but became a Christian in the first month there. It was God's love, accepting him, that impressed him. He said, 'Every day when I read the Bible it seemed that God highlighted His love for me.' In the security of that love he pursued his scientific research and then was called to the ordained ministry. He wrote:

It has been my privilege for nearly forty years to discover more of the amazing love of God. I have experienced that love of God in times of joy and sorrow, in success and failure, in strength and weakness. I know that God loves me. I know that my illness will give more opportunities to discover the riches of God's love.

So the foundations of God's love were deeply set. 'What about now?' I asked.

It would be foolish to pretend that it has been easy to accept the growing impact of my illness. Inability to keep up with the physical demands of a challenging and rewarding ministry pushes you towards despair. Stepping down from that ministry through early retirement challenges your sense of identity and purpose. The 'bad days' when you struggle to walk can leave you weeping with frustration. Fingers which refuse to obey your directions on the keyboard are exasperating. It has not been easy, but many other people face far greater disabilities.
Despite all the difficulties, and with the awareness that these

difficulties will increase in the years ahead, I remain confident of the Lord's unfailing love for me. I see the difficulties as the Lord's wise provision of opportunities to discover more of the riches of His love and grace. I do believe that the Lord is powerful to heal, but I face the awesome mystery of the 'now and not yet' of the kingdom of God.

It is thought-provoking that the text from Ephesians 3 quoted on page 82 is followed immediately by 'Now to him who is able to do immeasurably more than all we ask or imagine, according to his power that is at work within us, to him be glory in the church' (Eph. 3:20–21). This suggests that the more we grasp the extent of God's love, the more our lives are able to be used to God's glory as part of His 'glory in the church'. Or as Richard Rohr puts it: 'When we are inside of great love, we have a much stronger possibility of surrendering our ego controls and opening up the whole field of life. Great love makes us willing to risk everything, holding nothing back.'[5]

When suffering actually opens up our hearts in greater compassion and love for others and causes a loosening of any self-pride and an increasing delight in God, it becomes a powerful witness. It attracts by selfless love (rather than repels by self-pity). It encourages and challenges lives. Love shines and conquers.

*   *   *   *   *

An architect pointed out to me that to see the length, breadth, height and width of a building accurately, one has to stand in its exact centre. There is, of course, so much to learn about God's love from the life of Jesus our Lord: His compassion for the needy, His apparent helplessness as He allowed himself to endure the Passion, His 'example' of laying down His life for others, His tenderness when meeting with the distraught Peter on the shores of Galilee after Peter's denial. However, the full dimensions and perspective of God's love can only be seen from the centre, that is the cross, or as John expresses it in 1 John 4:10: 'This is love: not that we loved God, but that he loved us and sent his Son as an atoning sacrifice for our sins.' It is in His dying in our place, carrying the sins of the world, being the atoning sacrifice that we see love to the uttermost. All dimensions of the love of God, for the Christian, emanate from the cross.

A Christian counsellor tells me that in seeking to help spiritually wounded people, she tries to enable them to see the depth of God's love in the cross, which can take a long time for some. She explains that this '... involves helping them to appropriate God's forgiveness. When people are enabled to reflect on God's compassionate love and grace they become more fully aware of their own worth in God's sight.' She has found the service of Holy Communion to be powerful in its outward signs, in the participation we make 'as we are forgiven and we recover a sense of belonging in Christ, when emotions such as anger, guilt and hurt are expressed to God.' She is concerned when some churches treat the service carelessly and structure is lost, and appreciative when churches make the service reverent and real, using Eucharistic prayers and sensitive worship songs, allowing those taking part to enter deeply into the meaning of the cross for them under the Holy Spirit's direction. She asks, 'How can we truly love and forgive others when we are not fully aware of our own worth in God's sight?' and then comments: 'The Eucharist is the unique way Christians partake of God's forgiving love and are restored. The love of God can be tangibly felt in a Christian fellowship where people are accepted, heard and encouraged in an appropriate way. There is individual and corporate strengthening and God's glory can be manifested.'

There are those who say that God cannot suffer. However, as Jürgen Moltmann writes, 'were God incapable of suffering ... then he would also be incapable of love ... the one who is capable of love is also capable of suffering, for he also opens himself to the suffering which is involved in love.'[6] John Stott reinforces this point in *The Cross of Christ*: 'In the real world of pain, how could one worship a God who was immune to it?'[7] So everything draws us to the cross. Here God suffers; here we find our God sharing with us in deep suffering and, in one sense, in the sufferings of the world. All arguments, questions and anger about suffering become silent at the foot of the cross. As

Archbishop William Temple once said: 'Some say there cannot be a God of love because, if there were … his heart would break. The Church points to the cross and says, "It did break."'

It is only when Paul has looked at sin, the atonement, the new life possible in Christ by the Spirit, that he comes to the wonderful climax of Romans 8. Here is the confidence in the love of God that is built deeply on the cross and the new relationship we have with God in Christ. Here is the statement of someone who has known trouble, suffering, persecution and danger in his life. This is where every Christian needs to be, as far as possible, *before* suffering comes:

> **'Who shall separate us from the love of Christ? Shall trouble or hardship or persecution or famine or nakedness or danger or sword? … No, in all these things we are more than conquerors through him who loved us. For I am convinced that neither death nor life, neither angels nor demons, neither the present nor the future, nor any powers, neither height nor depth, nor anything else in all creation, will be able to separate us from the love of God that is in Christ Jesus our Lord' (Rom. 8:35–39, emphasis mine).**

NOTES

1   Michael Mayne, *The Enduring Melody* (London: Darton Longman and Todd, 2006), p.4.
2   My book *Grace People: Rooted in God's Covenant Love* (Milton Keynes: Authentic, 2006) expands this theme through the Bible.
3   Frances Young, *Face to Face* (London: Epworth Press, 1985) p.41.
4   John P. Benson served most of his ministry in Singapore; he was also Dean of Cambodia at one time. I am grateful to him for his contribution.
5   Richard Rohr, OFM, 'Opening the door: great suffering and great love', in *Radical Grace*, Center for Action and Contemplation, Albuquerque. My warm thanks.
6   Jürgen Moltmann, *The Crucified God* (London: SCM, 1974), pp.222–230.
7   John R.W. Stott, *The Cross of Christ* (Leicester: IVP, 1986).

ELEVEN

Increasing in hope as
an anchor for the soul

... that you may overflow with hope by the power of the Holy Spirit.
(Romans 15:13)

The aged peer walked towards me in the House of Lords. 'There is nothing left to hope for,' he said. It was an extraordinary statement, said without any greeting. I swallowed hard, prayed an 'arrow' prayer, and then replied 'But, in Christ, there is everything to hope for.' He paused, and grunted a 'Well, yes.' We began to talk about the way hope in Christ can change lives.

Having hope or lacking hope can affect a sufferer enormously. 'Ted' was our neighbour. He lived alone and was a good friend. He had a church connection but not, it seemed, a personal relationship with Christ. He bravely coped with increasing illness, even when he was 'imprisoned' in his top floor flat (it had no lift). He then went into hospital. The ward was modern and pleasant. He was happy while he thought he could be made well by the hospital, but he had always feared going into a geriatric ward. One day, after I had visited him, the staff told me (as Ted had no close relative anywhere near London), 'He is being moved into the old people's ward tonight.' I expressed my great concern that they must prepare him and warn him about this. They didn't – he was moved without warning. The phone rang that evening in our home. It was Ted. 'It's happened, Michael, it's happened,' he said, in a distressed voice. I went to see him as soon as I could. He was in a modern single room with a great view, but that did not seem to matter. His whole character had changed; despair had enveloped him. In spite of his church connection and our sharing from Scripture, he lacked any hope. He died within two weeks.

Doctors confirm that our state of mind plays a huge part in both illness and recovery, whether fearing the worst or hoping for the best. People thinking only of themselves and their symptoms take longer to recover than those who also consider others and appreciate how relatively 'blessed' they themselves may have been in the midst of suffering or hardship. A positive attitude aids recovery, whereas anxiety or depression frequently hamper progress or may lead to imaginary symptoms.

The hospital TV series *Casualty* provided some useful input on the subject. When the senior consultant was facing terminal illness from an 'inoperable' brain tumour, the scriptwriters gave him these words to say: 'I realise how fragile life is, so I have decided to make a choice – I choose hope.' A medic treating a casualty trapped in a vehicle because of a road accident or under debris following an earthquake will seek to buoy up the hope of the victim as well as treat them medically. One rugby-caused paraplegic goes for an assisted suicide because he has no hope, while another is full of hope as he speaks of his joy in each new morning, of the smell of a barbecue, of the sights of sunlight in the trees. Hope and despair powerfully affect us as human beings.

As said poignantly from the seemingly hopeless prison situation in *The Shawshank Redemption*, you 'get busy living or get busy dying'.

Hope does not ease pain. Most books written by those going through suffering make this point. Hope can inspire and assure, but it does not take the pain away, ease the discomfort or stop the body's advancing incapacity. It does not lessen the physical impact of chemotherapy. It does not stop us weeping in bodily frustration, or as we care for a dying loved one, or in bereavement. Yet hope is still there underneath, and acts as a gentle touch on our soul and spirit.

On the other hand, we are warned against self-pity. John Stott once said to me, when he became extremely frail and no longer able to move unaided, 'Michael, I am determined not to wallow in self-pity.' At another time, he reiterated that, whatever state he was in, he would be 'content' (Phil. 4:12). Michael Mayne wrote: 'Self-pity is an unattractive, negative emotion.'[1] Michael Wenham, writing as motor neurone disease consumed his body, tells how he sought to put a 'mute' in the mouth of self-pity, and went on: 'It is no good harbouring such negative thoughts. For one thing, such thinking is essentially self-indulgent and destructive; and, for another, it makes you a misery to be around.'[2] He resolved to allow himself no more than five minutes of self-pity a day! When Mike Harding,[3] was dying of cancer, he wrote: 'There is no room for "selfishness" nor indeed for "self-pity"; for, perhaps, the one and only thing which is virtually guaranteed to cut us off completely from the love of God is wallowing in the trough of self-pity. Self-pity, after all, is nothing more than a reflection of "self-pride".'

Hope is not just about eternity but also about life now. Dr Martin Luther King, who fought for the rights of non-whites in the USA in the 1950s and 1960s, came from a church tradition where cries of 'Hallelujah!' and 'Praise the Lord!' were commonplace, and the hopes of the congregation were regularly uplifted by singing Spirituals. But this did not make Dr King so heavenly minded that he was no earthly use. It fired him to act with hope and dynamic courage. Any whiff of self-pity was swept away, and any priority given to self-preservation was set aside. Hope fired him.

In 2008, Elim Christian School in Auckland, New Zealand, lost six of its senior students and one teacher when they were drowned in a freak accident during an adventure course. There was widespread and profound sympathy for the parents and family of those who had died. Questions as to how a loving God could possibly allow this to happen to such lovely teenagers were also thrown from all directions. The public expected the reaction to be one of anger overcoming faith, and blame overcoming forgiveness. But what came forth from the staff and students was a sure hope in resurrection, and this powerfully pervaded the memorial service. The youngsters told of their hope in Christ as their guide in this life and the next, and were stimulated by this event to dedicate their lives even more to Him. In the light of this witness, the Coroner's Court made an exception and allowed a prayer for healing, reconciliation and hope to be offered by the father of one of the girls who died.[4]

*   *   *   *   *

Hope at the human level is sustained with warm memories of past years, perhaps video recordings of those years, conversational reminiscences and laughter ('A cheerful heart is good medicine' – Prov. 17:22). David Watson said that he enjoyed watching comedy films, especially *The Pink Panther* films.

Hope is also expressed by keeping activity and interest in life as long as our bodies can cope. In 2007, posters on the London Underground read 'Rosie was diagnosed with the fatal disease MND. She has just been found floating down the river'. The picture showed Rosie Fraser, aged forty-four, at the helm of a sailing dinghy.[5]

We can also be lifted through thinking about 'whatever is true, whatever is noble, whatever is right, whatever is pure, whatever is lovely, whatever is admirable' and about anything that is 'excellent or praiseworthy' (Phil. 4:8).

Thanksgiving is another way that our spirit can be re-orientated. It permeated the prayer of a soldier at the outbreak of the First World War, as he faced the likely possibility of death: '... to have given me self-consciousness for an hour, in a world so breathless for beauty, would have been enough. But you have preserved it in me for 20 years and more – and so, come what may, I thank you and bless your name.'

The following anonymous poem, which appears in various versions and adaptations, was a great help to Bob Mortimer in his fight against cancer:

Cancer is so limited
It cannot cripple love
It cannot shatter hope
It cannot corrode faith
It cannot eat away peace
It cannot destroy confidence
It cannot kill friendship
It cannot shut out memories
It cannot silence courage
It cannot invade the soul
It cannot reduce eternal life

It cannot quench the Spirit
It cannot lessen the power of the resurrection

*   *   *   *   *

For the Christian, hope moves into an eternal dimension. We know, like any human being, that human hopes can be dashed as well as fulfilled, not least the hopes of being healed from a serious illness, but we also know that hope in Christ can *never* be dashed. Human hope is uncertain. That is why 'positive thinking' is helpful as far as it goes, but is actually inadequate and often damaging when without hope in Christ. Hope in Christ is 'sure' and 'certain' (Heb. 11:1).

The actual word 'hope' doesn't sound 'certain' because of the way it is used in daily life, as in 'hope the train comes on time' and 'hope I get good results'. The only reason the word is used in Scripture is because 'hope that is seen is no hope at all. Who hopes for what he already has?' (Rom. 8:24). However, it is transformed in Scripture into 'certain hope'. In 2 Corinthians 5:4–5, for example, we are told that being 'clothed with our heavenly dwelling' is *guaranteed* by the Spirit, and in John 14:2 our Lord doesn't just say, 'I am hoping to prepare a place for you' but rather 'I am *going* ... to prepare a place for you.'

'Hope' is referred to very many times throughout the New Testament. It lifts our eyes and our spirits. Like Christian in *The Pilgrim's Progress*, the glimpses of the 'beautiful mountains' of heaven ahead encourage us to go on. A famous British preacher back in the 1950s, Canon Guy King, used to say that if he wrote a chorus it would be Go on, Go on, Go on, Go on, Go on ...' Of course, anyone can do that with stoic grit and perhaps feeling hard done by, but the Christian, even when needing endurance to carry on, can do so with the inspiration of hope, with an eternal goal ahead.

We are taken by surprise when, after reading Paul's declaration in Romans 4:24–5:5 that because of our Lord's death for us on the cross and His resurrection from the dead we can be justified by faith, have peace with God, access into God's grace and hope of the glory of God, Paul goes straight on with 'Not only so, but we also rejoice in our sufferings'. The phrase leaves us open-mouthed. 'Rejoice in our sufferings? But why?' we ask. Because, Paul explains, '... suffering produces perseverance; perseverance, character; and character, hope.' So here we see a progression from rejoicing, and perhaps singing numerous choruses about the benefits to us of the gospel, to suffering. Hope becomes more real, more meaningful, more precious to us through suffering. Worship also becomes more important when 'Through all the changing scenes of life, in trouble and in joy, the praises of my God shall still my heart and tongue employ.'[6]

In earlier years, there were three symbols for Christianity: the dove, the fish and the anchor. We still use the first two frequently, but seldom use the anchor. It would be good to bring it back into use, to remind us that 'We have this hope as an anchor for the soul, firm and secure' (Heb. 6:19), and that because of this hope, we are to be 'greatly encouraged' (Heb. 6:18). Indeed, we should! Some will remember the chorus (usually sung with thumping vigour!):

> *We have an anchor that keeps the soul*
> *Steadfast and sure while the billows roll,*
> *Fastened to the Rock which cannot move,*
> *Grounded firm and deep in the Saviour's love.*[7]

Like that chorus, Romans 5:5 brings us back to love: 'And hope does not disappoint us, because God has poured out his love into our hearts by the Holy Spirit, whom he has given us.' So, all the way, our faith and our hope is matched by His love.

Our eyes are lifted and our assurance boosted in the second half of Romans 8. Although the creation is subject to 'frustration', this subjection is 'in hope' and this hope is 'that the creation itself will be liberated from its bondage to decay and brought into the glorious freedom of the children of God' (Rom. 8:21). Paul bids us look to 'the redemption of our bodies. For in this hope we were saved' (Rom. 8:23–24). Right from the start of this great scripture sequence, Paul says, 'I consider that our present sufferings are not worth comparing with the glory that will be revealed in us' (Rom. 8:18). Eyes up;

perspective right; hope burning; expectation alive!

No wonder Joni Eareckson Tada, an outstanding Christian and a quadriplegic, gets an enthusiastic response when she picks up the theme of 'the redemption of our bodies' and says to people like herself, 'One day we will walk and jump and run again'. The Christian hope lifts us to a new dimension of great anticipation – new resurrection bodies; the old will have gone; the new will have come. What a prospect for every believer, but especially for those whose bodies are restricted in this life.

*   *   *   *   *

I recall speaking to several hundred gifted women leaders at a meeting in the USA. Every woman was very well dressed, expertly made-up and with splendid hairstyles. I was expounding 2 Corinthians and came to 4:16: 'Therefore we do not lose heart. Though outwardly we are wasting away, yet inwardly we are being renewed day by day.' I looked them in the eye and had delight in saying: 'My dear friends, each of you is in irreversible decay!' There was a loud gasp!

The key to fighting decay is not just by outward daily treatment, but by inward renewal, day by day. How else do you explain a ninety-three-year-old retired clergyman, frail and thin, thanking me, his eyes streaming with tears: 'Thank you for what you have shown me about Jesus tonight.' This dear Australian man was clearly still being renewed every day, still open to hear and to learn even from a youngster, as I was then. Paul goes on to explain what stimulates that renewal. It is that 'our light and momentary troubles are achieving for us an eternal glory that far outweighs them all' (2 Cor. 4:17). Those enduring long debilitating illness may find the word 'momentary' hard to say, but they can still experience renewal every day. Further advice follows in 2 Corinthians 4:18: 'So we fix our eyes not on what is seen, but on what is unseen. For what is seen is temporary, but what is unseen is eternal.' What a boost! What a perspective! What an encouragement in our sufferings. Hope is to abound in us.

Malcolm Muggeridge powerfully and movingly expressed this

hope, this clinging on to God and finding his right hand upholding us, in these words:

> It is precisely when every earthly hope has been explored and found wanting, when every possibility of help from human sources has been sought and is not forthcoming, when every recourse this world offers, moral as well as material, has been explored to no effect, when in the shivering cold the last faggot has been thrown on the fire and in the gathering darkness every glimmer of life has flickered out – it is then that Christ's hand reaches out, sure and firm, that Christ's words bring inexpressible comfort, that his light shines brightest, abolishing the darkness for ever. So, finding in everything only deception and nothingness, the soul is constrained to have recourse to God himself and to rest content on him.[8]

What a sadness it is to be without this hope. It is said that when Sigmund Freud lost his twenty-one-year-old daughter in a flu epidemic shortly after the First World War, and then his four-year-old granddaughter, he saw that 'as the deepest of unbelievers' he had no one to accuse, no one to comfort him, and wrote these sad words: 'I am alone.'

Hope inspires us and encourages us, whatever the state of our lives – whether suffering or not. We have mainly mentioned personal suffering so far, but we know that many Christians suffer terrible persecution, homelessness and poverty in some parts of the world; we put our arms around them in love, praying for and taking action for their relief, but also praying that their faith may hold, their experience of God's love may become deeper, and that hope may sustain their spirits. The passage of Scripture with which we end this chapter will be even more meaningful to those who are in poverty and homelessness, but it is the hope of *every* believer. It stimulates us to see hope in terms of life, not death, as we head towards the new creation where:

Never again will they hunger;
never again will they thirst:
The sun will not beat upon them,
nor any scorching heat.
For the Lamb at the centre of the throne
will be their shepherd;
he will lead them to springs of living water.
And God will wipe away every tear from their eyes.
(Rev. 7:16–17)

NOTES

1 Michael Mayne, *The Enduring Melody*, (London: Darton Longman and Todd, 2006), p.209.

2 Michael Wenham, *My Donkey Body*, (Oxford: Monarch, 2008), p.76. See Chapter 10 note 4 of this book.

3 Mike Harding was a priest in the East End of London. This extract by him was written as he was dying, published in *Theology* Journal and reprinted here by kind permission of Celia Harding. (Date of issue not known.)

4 I am grateful to Bishop Peter Atkins for drawing this to my attention, and to the Principal of Elim Christian College in Auckland NZ for permission to include this. The tragedy happened on 16 April 2008.

5 Quoted by Michael Wenham in *My Donkey Body*, op.cit. p.153.

6 'Through All the Changing Scenes of Life', Nahum Tate (1652–1715) and Nicholas Brady (1659–1726) from Psalm 34.

7 'We Have an Anchor', Priscilla J. Owens (1829–1907).

8 Malcolm Muggeridge gave the 1967 London Lectures at All Souls, Langham Place, London on the theme 'Christ and the Media'. The words quoted are from the end of his third lecture.

TWELVE
The turning to a purpose

'You're in the team, Baughen!'

'But I'm not sure I ... '

'You can't be in this school and not be in a team!'

My inglorious cricketing 'career' was about to begin ...

'You're in the team!' says our Lord to every Christian. There is no such thing as 'individual' Christianity. We receive great benefits when we come to Christ, including eternal benefits and help in our daily lives, not least in suffering. But while Christianity is only 'there for us' and Christ is 'there for us', our faith is also self-centred. We have to take the step to call Him 'Lord', which turns us round and makes our faith become Christ-centred. Only then do we begin a new life of commitment in His team, a life in which we are called to pull our weight as best we can, to advance His purposes for the world and humankind, and to be His witnesses.

This helps to put all suffering into a new perspective. A fellow bishop, learning of the 'brickbats' and questions I was tackling in this book, said, 'There is one more question to add: "Why are Christians surprised by suffering?"' 1 Peter 4:12–13 says, 'Dear friends, do not be surprised at the painful trial you are suffering, as though something strange were happening to you. But rejoice that you participate in the sufferings of Christ ...'

Paul, in Philippians 1:29 even says, 'For it has been granted to you on behalf of Christ not only to believe on him, but also to suffer for him'. By witnessing to Christ in a world hostile to Him, we may add to our suffering, as so many of our brothers and sisters across the world know when they are persecuted for their faith.

My cricketing 'career' was not a success. I have no eye-to-ball co-ordination, and my aim as a young boy when I was batting was to survive the onslaught of that hard ball, usually by trying to block the ball. Some would endeavour to hit it, and some would strike it with courage and verve, scoring 'fours' and 'sixes'. As a Christian, we can choose to be those who simply survive, those who try to score a few runs, or those who endeavour to strike the ball 'for six'. The apostle Paul was clearly a striker 'for six'. He was playing for the Captain of the team, and for the honour of the Captain and the team, not for himself. He saw suffering as a sharing in Christ's sufferings, as an arena of witness to Christ and the gospel, and a means of spiritual growth.

Once, when Archbishop Donald Coggan was saying goodbye to an ordinand who had been to see him, the ordinand said to him, 'Take care!' He responded: 'Take risks!' In other words, we need to understand that the watchword is not 'self-preservation' but 'self-dedication'.

In the powerful first chapter of Philippians it is not suffering or death that occupies Paul's mind as he sits in prison, it is uplifting Christ: 'I eagerly expect and hope that I will in no way be ashamed, but will have sufficient courage so that now as always Christ will be exalted in my body, whether by life or by death' (Phil. 1:20).

Like many others, my wife Myrtle and I seek to make that prayer our own, facing the unknown of old age. There may come a time when all one can do is hold on and the days of a physically active life are over, but that does not need to lessen our aim to glorify Christ. Myrtle's mother became totally blind in her older years and eventually, in her late nineties, she could not cope any more with operating talking books, CD players and the like. So she spent much of her day in praying, particularly for people, and remembering them by praying alphabetically from A to Z. This was now the only way she could go on serving her Lord. She never complained. She delighted in Christian worship and teaching and in news of Christ's kingdom being advanced. Her love and grace glowed to the end, to the glory of Christ her Saviour.

The same perspective as Paul's is seen when the apostles faced opposition and imprisonment in Acts 4. After their release, they gathered the Church to pray (v.24); however, they did not ask their 'Sovereign Lord' for safety or protection but for the forwarding of the gospel: '... enable your servants to speak your word with great boldness' (Acts 4:29). God's purpose was what really mattered to them.

Our Lord warns of the sufferings that may come in Christian witness. In John 15:18,20, Jesus warns, 'If the world hates you, keep in mind that it hated me first. ... If they persecuted me, they will persecute you also.' These warnings are to prepare us, not to deter us. The purpose of discipleship is not to be deflected by such opposition. Christ's mission and His glory are too important.

Many of us can think of those who have risked and even lost their lives trying to share the gospel with those who have never even heard of Jesus. George Selwyn, for instance, who became the first Church of England Bishop of New Zealand in 1841, went frequently by sailing ship to share the good news with the people of the Solomon Islands, despite knowing that they were cannibals. Later, the first man to be appointed Bishop of the Islands was beheaded. Like so many other mission-centred believers, they understood that suffering is secondary to the purpose of mission for Christ. Indeed, suffering and martyrdom have often in themselves been powerful testimonies to Christ and to the advancement of His kingdom.

When he wrote '... greatly rejoice, though ... you may have had to suffer grief in all kinds of trials ... so that your faith ... may be proved genuine and may result in praise, glory and honour when Jesus Christ is revealed' (1 Pet. 1:6–7), we see how much Peter understood how powerful a witness suffering can be. He knew that spiritual growth, not physical comfort, was the key.

Romans 8:28–30 is often slightly misquoted as 'all things work together for good for those who love God' and is applied to our personal benefit. But if we look at the context of that phrase, from verse 18 to the end, we will see that it is about suffering and about the good, not my good. The sentence adds that it refers to those who also are '... called according to his purpose'. The passage is lifting us from self-preservation to self-dedication. It is our very suffering that can be turned to God's good purpose of spreading His gospel and His kingdom. It is to be seen as part of His purposes (and that is so reassuring), and verse 29 shows that part of His purpose is our growth in holiness 'to be conformed to the likeness of his Son'. All whose testimonies we have included in this book have the desire to glorify God even in the midst of painful personal suffering. They have their perspective right.

Many years ago, I was on a beach in the Isle of Man. As part of our Christian Youth Holiday activities, a vigorous beach hockey game was taking place. Angela, at seventeen, was a fine young Christian. She loved Romans 8:28, 'in all things God works for the good', and understood its meaning. In the midst of the game, she was smashed in the mouth and lost several front teeth, an awful thing for a seventeen-year-old. Her mouth was swollen and bloody, but as she went into the ambulance she managed to say through her swollen lips 'Romans 8:28!' She had no concern for herself. As a result of the way she took that smash, two girls came to faith in Christ, and some thirty years later I met one of them, now a fine Christian woman. 'I was one of those girls,' she said. Then she introduced her husband and family, all strong members of the church.

Hebrews 12:4–13 explains that hardships can act as a 'discipline', and that this is '... for our good, that we may share in his holiness'. It speaks of the 'harvest of righteousness and peace' that emerge from this 'training'. If we take away the idea of discipline as punishment and see it rather as a loving way for a parent to get a child on the right track, it helps us to take this text on board.

*   *   *   *   *

For me, the greatest help on suffering has been 2 Corinthians. It is the most passionate letter of the New Testament. It bursts into the theme of suffering. The passion burns in a life that has known more suffering than most of us will ever know, and it glows with the deepening closeness to God that has resulted from it. So, from the heart, Paul writes in 2 Corinthians 1:3–4: 'Praise be to the God and Father of our Lord Jesus Christ, the Father of compassion and the God of all comfort, who comforts us in all our troubles'.[1] He does not rest on that, but goes on to show the purpose for God that has come out of it:

'... the sufferings of Christ flow over into our lives, so also through Christ our comfort overflows' (2 Cor. 1:5). So now he can comfort others. He can bring the same sort of comfort that God has given him. His distress was actually for their benefit, as it has shown Paul how better to comfort them and to help them endure the same sufferings patiently ... A railway illustration might help. A railway terminus is where the lines terminate. Many want to treat comfort similarly. The comfort they receive is all that matters to them – full stop. Paul transforms this. His thinking is, for me, like a railway junction where lines are coming in from various directions and going out in several directions. In other words, whatever suffering comes to him, he sees the comfort he receives as something to go out from him too; he is to learn from God's comfort and to share it with others for their benefit. Although it helps, of course, when we have been through the same illness or problem and can truthfully say 'I know what you're feeling', Paul's text teaches us that the lessons of God's comfort to us can be applied in all directions.

> **Amy Carmichael said: 'I have noticed that when one who has not suffered draws near to one in pain, there is rarely much power to help.'**

> **An old Arab proverb says: 'All sunshine makes a desert.'**

In 2 Corinthians 1:8–9, Paul learns lessons from suffering that strengthen his own faith. We do not know what his experience was, except that he obviously thought, 'This is the end.' We sometimes use the phrase 'the bottom dropped out of my life'. We may see that in terms of redundancy, illness, financial problems, loss of a loved one, or even facing imminent death. Hopefully, however, we will be able to ask, with Paul, 'What can I learn from this?' For Paul, 'this happened that we might not rely on ourselves but on God, who raises the dead.'

Myrtle and I experienced something of this a few years ago. 'Prepare for crash landing!' shouted the captain of the aircraft. He had told us earlier that the plane had lost its hydraulics and their back-up. As the runway came into sight with the ambulances and fire engines at the ready, Myrtle and I held hands, prayed and each found ourselves imbued with total peace, indeed a peace that passed understanding – a *wonderful* experience. We survived. We learnt. Our trust in God (and our assurance of heaven ahead) was permanently deepened.

Even when the Corinthian church gets itself in a mess over a moral problem (see 1 Cor. 5 and 2 Cor. 2), Paul is restless with concern until he gets news from Titus, who has taken his message to them. Paul sees a good outcome at the end. In 2 Corinthians 7:9–11, he rejoices that his message to them of correction and guidance had brought deep sorrow and repentance, as well as alarm, longing, concern and a readiness to see justice done. It was painful to tackle the situation but the outcome was a huge encouragement. To have avoided the pain would have been a disaster for the church.

When our overall desire is to do God's will, to glorify Him and to advance the gospel, then suffering ceases to be central in our thinking, even though it still hurts, and His purposes in and through our lives and suffering become central to our living and the motivation of our worshipping hearts. We pray with Paul to 'have sufficient courage so that now as always Christ will be exalted in my body, whether by life or death' (Phil. 1:20).

NOTE
1 The word used for 'comfort' means 'coming alongside' and is the same word as is used for the 'Comforter', the Holy Spirit, in John's Gospel.

THIRTEEN

The theatre of God's power and grace

'Our lives are the theatre in which God's grace is displayed.'[1] These words triggered my mind to think about suffering. Non-believers may not read the Word of God but can read the lives of believers. If a Christian appears to be strong, healthy and successful, then non-believers may say, 'It's easy for them to believe in God' but when a radiant faith is seen in sufferers, then their witness is powerful and challenging.

There is a dramatic surprise after Paul has exulted (in 2 Cor. 4:6) about the glory of God shining in our hearts. The next verse begins with a 'But'. The glorious truth of 'Christ in us' is seen as set in fragile human bodies. So he says 'But we have this treasure in jars of clay ...' One can hardly conceive a greater contrast! Clay jars are so fragile; they crack or break if dropped. So is the human frame. We are carbon-based beings, subject to illnesses, diseases, decay and death. Yet Christ is in us!

Why such a contrast? Paul blows open our minds to see why: 'to show that this all-surpassing power is from God and not from us' (v.7). We are to be the theatre of grace; people who can be seen to glow with the indwelling grace and glory of Christ, even in suffering. We are to be living testimonies to the power of God within us. We now have a theology of suffering. Christ is glorified in the context of our suffering and the way we handle it. We have the same illnesses, diseases and disasters as non-believers, but there is a huge difference. We meet suffering with Christ in us, alongside us and around us. If, because we were Christians we were freed from all suffering, the most powerful witness to the reality of Christ in us would more or less disappear. So instead of resisting, we should take suffering up into the purpose of God for our lives as His children and His witnesses. This is God's intention.

Driving down the M4 motorway on the way to expound 2 Corinthians at a church weekend in the West Country, I read the words 'Utterly Butterly' on a huge lorry as we slowly overtook it. 'That's it!' I thought. 'That's 2 Corinthians 4:8!' The verse, of course, that follows the clay jars verse: 'We are hard pressed on every side, but not crushed; perplexed, but not in despair; persecuted, but not abandoned; struck down, but not destroyed' ('knocked down but ... [not] knocked out' in J.B. Phillips' version, italics mine). Paul spells out the power of witness in suffering. We are 'but' people because of the grace of God.

When Stephen was being stoned to death in Acts 7:54–60, the power of his testimony in words, his looking to Christ and his praying for forgiveness for his murderers obviously penetrated the heart of Saul the persecutor, who witnessed it all and for whom it could well have been one of the major causes of his conversion.

When I asked a young person why she was turning to Christ, she pointed to a couple in the church and said: 'It was the way they took the cot death of their child that convinced me there must be a God, and I began to seek Him.'

As a theological student, I took part in a mission. It took place out of the church to which a fellow student belonged, and his family were kind enough to let me stay in their home. His father was a Salvation Army officer, racked with asthma and almost at death's door. Christ glowed in him. Every night when we came home, he eagerly awaited news of the mission; his eyes shone even as he choked and breathed the vapours from the bowl to ease his discomfort. Suffering? No thought of it! His whole concern was Christ's mission. He powerfully affected my life.

In Acts 16:22–25 we read that Paul and Silas, stripped, beaten and flogged, in the inner cell of a dingy prison in Philippi, feet fastened in the stocks, were praying and singing hymns to God – even at midnight! When an earthquake struck and the doors of their cell flew open, their first thought was to care for their jailer. No wonder the man sought salvation and was baptised, together with his whole family.

One night in 1978, a probation officer called Arthur Caiger opened the door of his home to a young man who threw hydrochloric acid in his face. He went blind as a result. Almost thirty years later, in 2007, he was attending a Study Week that I was leading in Keswick. I was so moved to see this man's radiant face and his delight in the Word of God, as well as the great love he (and his wife) had for God and everyone around them. He told me that it had not been easy at first to forgive his attacker, but when he did so, he found his heart 'flooding with God's peace'. While he was recovering from the incident in hospital, a reporter from a national newspaper came to interview him. 'How can you still believe in the love of God?' she asked him. He told her of what God's love meant to him. He had been 'knocked down' but clearly not 'knocked out'! The reporter, taken aback, apparently left the hospital totally perplexed by his answer. Ever afterwards, Arthur's life was a powerful theatre of God's power and grace. The treasure shone through his blindness and his clay jar![2]

In the summer of 1989, during the communist regime, the following amazing headline appeared in a Hungarian daily newspaper:

AN ANGEL FLIES INTO BUDAPEST
MIRACLE IN THE PEOPLE'S STADIUM

The newspaper was reporting on a gathering of 90,000 Christians at a Budapest stadium. The meeting had been organised by Billy Graham, but it was Joni Eareckson Tada who 'stole the show'.[3] Some twenty years before, Joni had dived into what proved to be all-too-shallow water, and emerged as a quadriplegic. As this wonderful Christian spoke from her wheelchair, she had a dynamic and riveting impact on the huge crowd (including the reporters from the communist newspaper) because of the testimony of her words and her life. Her faith was so obviously real. The miracle was not of her healing, which would have been a one-time event, but of her faith and courage, which had been a lifetime miracle! She has not wallowed in self-pity, but has put her life into God's hands to use – and how marvellously He has used it! Whenever I have listened to her speak, I have always been deeply thankful to God for her 'knocked down but not knocked out' attitude.

Another example of God's grace at work was when, in 2005, Abigail Witchalls[4] was stabbed in the neck and left paralysed, the media were rightly amazed at her courage. Her faith has been strong and evident. As some sensation began to return to her body she said, 'God is doing beautiful things' (a phrase that was headlined by the press) – what a witness! In 2009 she went to Lourdes, and asked God to heal her 'in the way I need most, according to your will'. She wrote: 'He did heal me, not physically – but he freed me to love life and to know daily the joy I longed for. To my surprise I find that I have more to give now that I'm paralysed than when I was able-bodied. This is one of God's little miracles.' What a God-glorifying testimony, and yet another example of being 'knocked down but not knocked out'.

As well as these high-profile examples, we could no doubt fill thousands more pages with examples of men and women, boys and girls, past and present, who have shown the power and grace of God in their lives in spite of suffering. We should also recall the testimonies of Christians suffering from wasting disease, motor neurone disease, terminal cancer, physical disablement and so much more, as well as Christians in our own local church whose lives shine through the brokenness of their clay jar of a body. Our daughter-in-law, Rachel, has had to face several years with chronic myeloid leukaemia. She was in the small percentage of those for whom the new drugs did not work. A stem cell replacement seems to be the only medical treatment. No match has been found out of 13 million possible donors. Yet her faith, her courage and her determination to continue serving Christ has been a very powerful testimony.

All of these people are marked by a steady faith, a pressing on in life and service for their Lord, and seeking His glory. As clay jars, they have accepted that the all-sufficient power is from God and not from themselves.

In 2 Corinthians 4:10, Paul gives suffering an even deeper dimension: 'We always carry around in our body the death of Jesus, so that the life of Jesus may also be revealed in our body.' In 2 Corinthians 1:5 he had said that 'the sufferings of Christ flow over into our lives'. Now in 2 Corinthians 4:10–11 he emphasises that the resurrection life in Christ should thus become more evident – the light of being risen with Christ shining through the fragile clay jar.

*   *   *   *   *

For most of us, suffering is not so stark and extreme, but we are still clay jars in the hurly-burly of daily life. Christians are not delivered from all suffering but face the same circumstances of life as everybody else, yet do so with Christ, with the treasure of His light within, the joy of a relationship with Him, our hand in His hand. It is that difference that we should show. We should glow for Christ. In 2 Corinthians 6:3–10, Paul gives us a torrent of applications. He calls us 'to commend ourselves in every way', not in terms of personal pride but 'as servants of God'. Each day is a new day to commend to God and to ask for His help as His servants and witnesses. If openings come to speak for Him, we will take them, but mostly we should handle anything that happens with the touch of Christ and with the grace of Christ. Paul lists the things that happen to us in life, particularly what we suffer because we are Christians, and the extra demands on us physically in the cause of the gospel. He then gives a list of the characteristics that are to mark out the Christian: 'purity, understanding, patience and kindness; in the Holy Spirit and in sincere love; in truthful speech and in the power of God; with weapons of righteousness in the right hand and in the left' (vv.6–7) whether we are in the office or factory, at college or school, in hospital, on the farm, at the sports club, wherever we go. In the same situations as others, we should glow. For instance, integrity is an increasingly valued mark of Christians in business and other walks of life. Paul uses the word 'pressures' several times in 2 Corinthians. It is something to which we all relate. We share them with everybody else, but we also have Christ sharing with us – and it should show!

The passage in 2 Corinthians 6 ends by describing two jibes at Christians (so up to date!) and then how we handle particular pressures:

> genuine, yet *regarded as* impostors;
> known, yet *regarded as* unknown;
> dying, and yet we live on;
> beaten, and yet not killed;
> sorrowful, yet *always* rejoicing;
> poor, yet making many rich;
> having nothing, and yet possessing everything.
> (2 Cor. 6:8–10, emphasis mine)

In other words, utterly yetterly Christians!

Possibly the most precious text for anyone facing the troubles of this life (and indeed even when not experiencing troubles) is 2 Corinthians 12:9. Paul says that when he pleaded with the Lord to take away the thorn in his flesh, the Lord replied, 'My grace is sufficient for you, for my power is made perfect in weakness.' Paul's response is not 'Well, I'll have to put up with it then!' like a stoical martyr. Instead, he takes it up and runs with it. He sees that it is not God's will to take this thorn from him, and immediately understands that it must be the Lord's will for him to take up his suffering for Christ's glory. Hence his 'therefore' statement: 'I will boast all the more gladly about my weaknesses, so that Christ's power may rest on me. That is why, for Christ's sake, I delight in weaknesses, in insults, in hardships, in persecutions, in difficulties. For when I am weak, then I am strong' (2 Cor. 12:9–10). His use of words like 'boast' and 'delight' takes one's breath away! As this is the way God is going to glorify Himself, Paul will *go* for it with all his energy. His suffering will make him a theatre of God's power and grace.

NOTES

1   Charles J. Ellicott, *Commentary on the Whole Bible* (Grand Rapids, MI: Zondervan, 1979; first published in 1884).

2   Arthur died in 2008. I am grateful to his widow, Ruth, for her permission to include this paragraph. Her letter glowed with love, peace and hope!

3   I am grateful to Dennis and Amy Loveless for giving me the newspaper cuttings about this day in Budapest. They were there and so witnessed it first-hand.

4   I appreciate the kindness of Abigail Witchalls in allowing me to quote her.

FOURTEEN
The touch of care

1 Peter 5:7 says He 'cares for' us. We see the way our Lord cares in the Gospels – His thoughtful care for the disciples in the storm, in the shock of John the Baptist's beheading, in bereavement care for Martha and Mary, in serving breakfast on the beach after the resurrection, in personal time with Peter after his denial. We see it in His care for the needy, the sick, the lame, the blind, the dumb, the lepers (including touching the untouchable); in His description of Himself as the caring Shepherd. We know it (and, no doubt, are often unaware of it) in our lives, with many touches of His love and ways in which things happen that seem only explicable as His caring intervention. 'Because he himself suffered ... he is able to help [us]' (Heb. 2:18). He is not a remote God, but One who has walked this very earth.

It is this same care that He expects to flow within the Church and from the Church. When He washed the disciples' feet, He then told them to wash one another's feet (John 13:1–17), and when He told the parable of the Good Samaritan, He told His hearers to go and do likewise (Luke 10:25–37). He commands us to 'Love each other (as He has loved us)' (John 15:12). The Church, at its best, should be a place of acceptance, of valuing each and every one regardless of background or health or education, with a special care for the sick and needy. It should be a community of love where 'If one part suffers, every part suffers with it' (1 Cor. 12:26). Matthew 25:31–46 separates those who care for the sick, the hungry, the thirsty, those without clothes and those in prison, but because they do this as a 'natural' part of their Christian living, they are surprised to be commended by the King. The others had never caught on. From the early years of the Church, Christians have been urged to show this care to everyone who is ill or in poverty or in prison. Caring initiatives by Christians led to the starting of schools, hospitals, almshouses, and later to attacking the slave trade and the terrible conditions in the factories and mines. Today, we see the same care expressed in aid funds, in hospices and in many other aspects of medical and social care.

I recall an elderly lady, small of stature, who lived at the end of a cul-de-sac in Manchester. She was a lovely member of the church, with a real faith. She was also known throughout the cul-de-sac as a person who loved, cared and supported, who would do what she could for anyone in need. She had the hands and heart of Christ. She truly fulfilled the command of Jesus to love our neighbour as ourselves, and not to hold back like the priest and the Levite in the story of the Good Samaritan (Luke 10:25–37). In that story only the Samaritan got involved, and his touch of care was practical, costly and without barriers. In contrast, in the same church as that caring elderly lady there were two students who seemed the keenest of Christians, but one day another resident of the hostel where the students lived came to tell me that while they were always ready to give out tracts, they were never there when care was needed.[1]

Another special person in that church was Bert Hollinshead. He was full of energy, with a vigorous Christian faith, and had been a prisoner of the Japanese from the fall of Singapore in the Second World War. He was in one of the notorious prison camps on the River Kwai. When men fell ill with dysentery and other weakening illnesses, they were separated from everyone else. The guards would not go near them. But Bert Hollinshead did. He so *cared* in the name of Christ that his own survival was secondary to outpoured love and practical action.

How should we minister care to those who suffer?

Obviously this will vary according to the situation. First of all, however, everyone should be treated with respect – we were *all* created in the image of God. The person in the wheelchair deserves to be given the same respect as the person wheeling the chair. The hospital patient should be addressed by name, not as 'the duodenal ulcer in bed six'. Mother Teresa insisted that caring should be with 'respect-love', and she cared for the poor in that way. Dame Cicely Saunders used to say that when our identity is disintegrating, we need to be heard and assured that our life has made sense and has been of value.

Once, towards the end of a Christian youth holiday I was leading, I went down with labyrinthitis (which causes vertigo). The world spun, and it was not possible for me to carry on ministering, so Myrtle and I went to a nearby Christian hotel for a break. I could not walk straight and found people treating me 'differently'. The next year we went back (in good health) to the same hotel, and I heard someone say 'Oh! He's quite intelligent, after all!' It was a salutary experience.

I asked Bob Mortimer to tell me the bad experiences of people visiting him. They included the following:

- *An older man saying to him 'It will make a man of you, boy!'*
- *A few people who tried to 'reassure' him by saying that the problem was probably not serious — which he found insulting.*
- *Some who talked incessantly about their own illnesses and symptoms, to the exclusion of all else.*
- *Others, with a broad smile, who could only quote Scripture verses as a panacea.*
- *Some who recounted amazing healing miracles and insisted, without any qualification or supporting evidence, that he should be expecting something similar.*
- *Some who were reluctant to mention the subject of cancer at all, though well aware of his situation.*
- *Conversely, others who talked about nothing else but the cancer, often in hushed tones, when his wish was to be treated as more than just a cancer sufferer.*
- *Some who struggled to cope with the situation — he had to help them out and try to make them feel better, which was exhausting.*

Dame Cicely Saunders, the founder of the first purpose-built hospice in the UK, and a leader in palliative care, said that patients chiefly wanted visitors to look as if they were trying to understand them. When we are visiting sufferers, it demands a concentration of mind to imagine ourselves in their situation. It is, of course, what the second great commandment requires, that we should love others *as we love ourselves*. Hebrews 13:3 says, 'Remember those in prison *as if you were their fellow prisoners*, and those who are mistreated *as if you yourselves were suffering*' (italics mine). That is true caring.

Some years ago, there was an advertisement on display in Euston Station. A boy's face was pictured, with these words:

> *Some people call me a mongol ...*
> *Others call me a Down's syndrome child ...*
> *My friends call me David.*

One of the blessings of places or occasions that are dedicated to prayer and healing for those who suffer is that there is total acceptance. There is time for personal care and prayer. They are not just a sufferer but a full person. The person in the wheelchair does not feel a 'nuisance'. The mentally ill are loved and accepted.

Care for full-time carers is part of the Church's love-responsibility. Looking after loved ones all the time, day and night, is immensely demanding. The physical demands are often exhausting. The mental demands with mentally ill loved ones can be overwhelming. So, members of the church who care for the carers by going to be with the person in need – enabling the carer to rest or go out – are acting with Christian love. Some people have well-hidden problems, and need deep counselling for these to be dealt with properly. One person who had a traumatic upbringing told me of a couple in her church who 'became Jesus' to her. When they first met one another, they just sat in complete silence because of the enormity of the memory that had surfaced. She said that the love, care, compassion and steadfastness that they showed was something she had never experienced before. Christian counselling is a specialised ministry, not to be undertaken without proper training. It is encouraging to know that more and more Christians are being trained in the skill. (One key part of such training is learning how to avoid being totally drained by someone who is demanding more frequent attention than is justified by their suffering.)

I also asked Bob Mortimer to tell me of the good experience of visitors. He gave me the following list:

- Those who were able to discuss his symptoms, progress, etc in a natural way, without awkwardness or embarrassment.
- Those who were willing to talk about other things too, recognising that he had a life apart from cancer.
- Those who were able to speak sensitively into his situation, whose spiritual contribution (eg words of Scripture) never sounded pious or forced.
- Those who were willing to pray not only for healing within the purposes of God, but also for strength and grace to cope with every new challenge and trial.
- Those who kept in regular contact, remembering and enquiring about results of scans and check ups.
- Those who had trodden a similar road, and could share helpfully from their own experiences. For example, one friend told him that she recited words of Scripture while undergoing radiotherapy treatment. He followed this advice during his own radiotherapy, incorporating scriptural songs and Bible passages such as Psalm 23, and found it a helpful and uplifting way of dealing with what could have been a depressing ordeal.
- Those who remembered to include his wife, Margaret, and his daughters in their prayers and support, recognising that they were sharing equally in the situation.

There are some situations when words do not help; for instance, in the midst of depression, when devastated in bereavement, when mentally under strain. When Elijah collapsed in spiritual depression after the great triumph of faith on Carmel and prayed that he might die, God did not answer him with words, but with an angel bringing 'a cake of bread baked over hot coals, and a jar of water' (1 Kings 19:1–9). Gentle words will follow much later. Sometimes a pie, a cake or a bunch of flowers are better than words. We need much sensitivity in visiting and caring.

John Westerhoff[2] tells the story of a disabled boy who was allowed to go to the local shop one day. His return was delayed, so his mother went to find him. His friend Carol had dropped her doll and it had broken. 'Did you stay to help her pick it up?' she asked. This was his reply: 'No, mother, I had to stay and help her cry.' The boy's memorable words go to the heart of care. Quite often, sharing others' crying is better than words. John 11:33–35 tells us that when Jesus reached the mourning Mary and 'saw her weeping' he was 'deeply moved ... and troubled'. Then we read: 'Jesus wept.' This is caring love.

Caring for those with mental illness

In a BBC Radio service, the Reverend Sharon Grenham-Toze[3] shared her experience of mental illness. Newly ordained and following a difficult personal experience, Sharon became mentally ill and spent some time in a mental hospital, where she experienced 'both the indignities and the stigma of mental illness'. What hurt her most was the falling away of several relatives and friends who could not cope with her illness. In that state she asked, 'Where is God?' Later, looking back, she could see many touches of His love through people. Gradually she came out of the illness and, like Elijah, she began to know the 'still small voice', as God brought her back. Now, many years on, she is exercising a full ministry, in full health of mind and body.

When I asked her 'What do those with mental illness value most in care?' she replied:

> I needed to be seen as me, a person still, not just an illness. It was best when people didn't 'hold me responsible' for my illness/misfortune. Those who kept in touch regularly by writing/sending cards helped me a great deal, because their words were something I could return to, especially if I had not been able to absorb them upon my first reading. When I was at home, the practical aspects of caring were important – so, someone who did the ironing when I felt overwhelmed; another who dropped round a cooked meal for me and the children ... being allowed to say and think negative things about God, without causing shock or an attempt to tell me

how wrong I was. (There were those who told me I was suffering because I didn't have enough faith, others who told me my illness was punishment for getting divorced!) Simply standing by me, staying in touch, refusing to give up on me or see me as 'failed' or 'scary', coming with me to appointments, keeping me in touch with events in the church/community when I was isolated in hospital ... helping me to feel I had not been forgotten or rejected by everyone.

Caring for the bereaved

Bereavement is always traumatic and, of course, experiences differ. Many will empathise with and be helped by the words of Mel Menzies:[4]

One of the things I learned when my daughter, Katya, died was that no matter how anticipated a death might be, it is nonetheless shocking. That surprised me! You may feel – as I did – that because you have rehearsed this death in your mind a thousand times, you're prepared for the event: immunised and buffeted against the trauma. The fact that you're not, makes it a 'double whammy'. When your expectation of preparedness is confounded, you learn the truth: the truth that the power of death is, humanly speaking, utterly devastating; utterly disempowering. And yet again, it is not! Because the second thing I learned was that no matter how it might seem, God remains faithful to His promises. This, perhaps, is the hardest thing for Christian and non-Christian to grasp. Strangely though – or perhaps not so strangely – it never crossed my mind to doubt.

Mel also wrote: 'God has His reasons. They may be mysteries beyond our comprehension. But I learned in my heart what I knew in my head: our faith is not in the outworking of His purposes, but in His personhood.'

She had to work through guilt and forgiveness; to deal with the 'need to lash out'; to treasure memories of her daughter. She wrote:

Moving on does not mean abandoning those you mourn. Nor does it mean leaving behind the pain of bereavement. In a corner of your heart a thorn resides. You may choose to allow it free rein so that it defines you for the rest of your life. Or you may choose, in God's grace to allow Him to wrap that thorn tenderly in His love. There it will remain, dormant and benign unless disturbed. It is a reminder of His immense suffering for us. And the hope we have in Him.

And what about ...?

There are, of course, many types of suffering that require our care, and it would take a separate book to write about them. Most of all, our care is acting in the name of Christ, acting with the love of Christ, even being Christ to others. This means we are to care with the compassion of Christ, we are to come alongside others to be with them. Caring also means helping one another to know that the Supreme Carer is with all who love Him, that His caring means He is with us always, whatever our feelings, and that He is also alongside and with all who care for others in His name, by His grace and Spirit, and with His love.

NOTES

1 Most of our crowd of students were not like that. They were very caring, and a number not only cared for fellow students, but also visited the needy and lonely in the parish.

2 John H. Westerhoff, *Spiritual Life: The Foundation for Preaching and Teaching* (Louisville, KY: Westminster John Knox Press, 1994), p.31. Brought to my notice by Canon Chris Burkett.

3 Sharon Grenham-Toze has now been ordained eleven years. She is currently working as a prison chaplain as well as being a regular broadcaster on BBC Radio 2 and 4. I am grateful for her readiness to write this piece.

4 One of Mel Menzies' books is called *A Painful Post Mortem* (Booklocker.com, 2008) and is endorsed by the Bereaved Parents Network. Obtainable from www.melmenzies. co.uk/books or bookshops. I appreciate her writing this piece for me.

FIFTEEN

The trust of prayer

My soul clings to you; your right hand upholds me. (Psalm 63:8)

As the father and his young son walked across the park, a huge storm hit – torrential rain and then hailstones. The father picked up the boy and ran for cover; the boy yelled with fright, but clung very closely to his father whose large hands held him tight.

For many, prayer in suffering is like that little boy's yell. In fear, possibly of the unknown, we may yell, sometimes even at God but, if we are secure in His love, we know we can trust Him; we know He is upholding us and that He will understand the turmoil of our emotions; we cling more tightly.

There are different forms of prayer,[1] but here we are concentrating on the very special experience of trusting prayer, when we are overwhelmed by suffering. For many it becomes a throwing of ourselves on God. One person has described it to me as like scraping off a picture that has been painted over a masterpiece; we have prayed to our concept of God (often well-informed by Scripture), but now our soul is laid bare, concepts are stripped away (especially necessary if we are still of the idea that God is only there to deliver what we ask for), and we are face to face with God Himself.

This is an experience that in grief can go beyond words. Paul surely knew it in the many sufferings of his life, for he writes in Romans 8:26 that in our weakness 'We do not know what we ought to pray for, but the Spirit himself intercedes for us with groans that words cannot express'. These are times when we may fall on our knees and, in tears, just hold on to God. It may be in silence. It may be as we walk alone or go to a quiet place just to draw nearer to God. There is also something deeper happening: '... he who searches our hearts knows the mind of the Spirit, because the Spirit intercedes for the saints in accordance with God's will' (Rom. 8:27). We hold on to the truth that God's purposes are bigger than ours, His thoughts higher than our thoughts, but most of all we hold on to God Himself, knowing He holds on to us. In such prayer we trust the Spirit, for He understands us and our sufferings better than we understand ourselves and, of course, knows God's overall will and purpose.

Towards the end of the book of Job, there are four whole chapters (Job 38–41) on God's tremendous revelation of Himself. Job's concept of God is blown apart as he is shown just how limited it is compared with the overwhelming reality of the glorious Creator God. Job's response is 'Surely I spoke of things I did not understand, things too wonderful for me to know. ... My ears had heard of you but now my eyes have seen you. Therefore I despise myself and repent in dust and ashes' (Job 42:3,5–6). In Job 42:7–16, the so-called friends are rebuked for false teaching, made to offer a sacrifice in Job's presence, and Job prays for them. The friends are spared because the Lord accepts Job's prayer; the Lord richly blesses Job.

When Nelson Mandela was a prisoner on Robben Island, he was brought the news that his son had been killed. It is reported that he went to the window of his cell and stood there in silence for four days. He refused food and refused to speak to anybody. We do not know what happened as he stood there, but those close to him believe he had been deeply communing with God. They observed that he emerged a greatly changed man, with release from bitterness and with a much deeper wisdom.

We do know that our Lord was in deep communion with His Father during the forty days of deprivation, hunger and physical suffering in the wilderness (Matt. 4:1–11), and at other times when He 'went off to a solitary place, where he prayed' (Mark 1:35) or when He went alone 'up on a mountainside to pray' (Mark 6:46). We also look in awe at His prayer in Gethsemane (Luke 22:40–46), the sweat as drops of blood, the deep open heart-cry to His Father, and the overriding readiness to do His Father's will. We look with greater awe at our Saviour suffering on the cross, crying, 'My God, my God, why have you forsaken me?' as He took our sins upon Him, knowing the awful sense of separation from His Father (Matt. 27:46). In the deepest agony of our heart, we will hopefully find strength and peace if we ponder the accounts of our Lord's passion and crucifixion, and will find encouragement to rest our lives, as He did, within the overall will of God, even when we do not understand the circumstances of our suffering and find it very difficult to bear.

Some years ago, there was a remarkable exhibition at the National Gallery in London, called 'Seeing Salvation'. It was a collection of paintings from different eras depicting, primarily, the crucifixion and the sufferings of Christ's passion. Myrtle and I went to it because we were nearby and thought we ought to see it. Our almost casual approach was immediately rebuked as we entered. We were unprepared for the impact it had on us and, it seemed, on the crowds viewing it. In spite of the numbers present, there was a deep hush, a reverent awe, a quietness that seemed to pervade the inner being. The organisers gave a hint as to why this was happening by stating that Bernard of Clairvaux (1090–1153), who wrote the hymn 'O Sacred Head Once Wounded', was the first to see the cross of Christ as a paradigm of human suffering. That was almost tangibly felt as people stood gazing at and pondering the pictures on display. Human suffering was seen through the lens of the self-giving love and sacrifice of the Suffering Servant, the Saviour of the world. Everyone left the exhibition in silence.

Our prayer to God is encouraged by Hebrews 4:16 where we are reminded that our Lord is able to sympathise with our weaknesses, because He has walked this same earth: 'Let us then approach the throne of grace with confidence, so that we may receive mercy and find grace to help us in our time of need.' Do we hear that? *With confidence*! He expects us to come, invites us to come, and we can do so with an open heart to tell Him exactly how we feel and what is overwhelming us. We do not come to tell Him what to do or to demand this or that solution to our needs. In Philippians 4:6 we are told 'Do not be anxious about anything, but in everything, by prayer and petition, with thanksgiving, *present* your requests to God' (italics mine). How often do children come and tell their parents their problems? They present them. They trust that their parents know best about what happens next.

> *Forgotten for eternity*
> *Is that to be my destiny?*
> *Your face no more to smile on me,*
> *Oppressed by every enemy,*
> *My soul enduring agony?*
> *Oh, answer me, my God!*
> *Oh, answer me, my God!*
>
> *Restore to me serenity*
> *And, in your gracious charity,*
> *Lest I should die, give light to me.*
> *Frustrate my gloating adversary,*
> *Uplift my soul in ecstasy,*
> *And I'll rejoice, my God!*
> *And I'll rejoice, my God!*
> *(Michael Saward)*[2]

The Psalms are often turned to as we come to God in need (eg 6,10,22,28,42,55). We feel an identity with the psalmist when he cries out in desperation and pain; when he feels desolate and abandoned. He is sometimes like the child who comes to his father and pummels his father's chest in frustration, yet then holds on in trust. The soul is laid bare; there is the honesty of the agonised heart.

Like an earthly father, our heavenly Father will understand. He also will want us to go deeper in trust. In the New Testament there is no pummelling of God, although the cry 'My God, my God ...' may well enshrine it for us. As New Testament Christians we see the Father, we see the depth of His love, we see things not in terms of material reward like the Old Testament (abundant harvests, plentiful fruit, a quiver full of sons) but in the 'bigger' spiritual and eternal terms – in terms of a relationship with God who blesses us for ever. So, although we may sometimes act like the psalmist, we need to grow in deeper trust and, instead of pummelling in frustration, lean closer on Him in silent trust and prayer.

> *In silence my soul is waiting,*
> *Is waiting for God alone,*
> *Deliverance from Him is coming*
> *My rescuer, fort and rock.*
> *In silence my soul is waiting*
> *Secure, I shall not be moved.*
> *(Michael Saward)*[3]

Most of the psalms that express pain and suffering also have praise within them, even Psalm 22, the 'My God, my God' psalm later has 'From you comes ... my praise in the great assembly' (v.25). And even in Psalm 42, which is about spiritual depression, the writer holds on to hope and praise in the last verse: 'Put your hope in God, for I will yet praise him, my Saviour and my God.' Philippians 4:6 also insists that we bring our requests 'with thanksgiving'. In praising and thanking Him, we turn the focus from ourselves to God; we put the balance right between our clinging to Him and His upholding of us.

We can also be deeply thankful, as Christians, that we are not alone. We do not have to carry the burden of suffering on our own. Not only do we have our heavenly Father, but we are part of God's family, the Church. Here should be a fellowship of support and prayer, where we do not have to put on a mask to hide our feelings, but can share in an atmosphere of trust and love. Like the men who let their friend down through the roof on a stretcher to the feet of Jesus (Mark 2:1–12), we may carry our brother or sister in prayer to His feet. In times when they are too ill to pray for themselves, the Church is to be their intercessor. We enfold them with our love and entrust them to our heavenly Father. We help them cling to God. We help them know that His right hand upholds them.

NOTES

1   My book on prayer is called *The Prayer Principle* (Fearn, Tain: Christian Focus
     Publications, 2007).
2   Michael J. Saward, version of Psalm 13 in *Psalm Praise* (Eastbourne: Falcon/Kingsway,
     1973). Copyright M.J. Saward. Used by his kind permission.
3   Michael J. Saward, first verse of his version of Psalm 62 in *Psalm Praise*, ibid.

SIXTEEN

Lord, take it away from me

To keep me from becoming conceited because of these surpassingly great revelations, there was given me a thorn in my flesh, a messenger of Satan, to torment me. Three times I pleaded with the Lord to take it away from me. (2 Corinthians 12:7–8)

The telephone rings: 'This is John. I am ringing to ask for your prayer. Mary has been diagnosed with cancer of the liver and the situation is serious.' 'Yes, of course we will pray.' We do so in our prayer times and add Mary (and John) to the urgent list …

A letter tells us of the unexpected illness of another friend and we are asked to pray. Of course, we do so. An email tells us of a Christian leader who has been in an accident, and is in a critical condition. 'Please pray,' is the request. Of course, we will do so …

Several beloved members of the church are facing serious illness and a special time to gather with them for prayer and laying on of hands is arranged. The sufferers are surrounded by love as well as held in prayer …

The staff team of the church is away at a conference when the news reaches us that a long-desired baby has been born with his life hanging by a thread. We meet at once for prayer and sense God is in this. We get back to the hospital and pray over him. Later the same day, the church meets for its normal prayer evening. We have a special time of prayer for this little baby. As we pray, he begins to respond …[1]

Two teenagers in the same church contract leukaemia around the same time. The church prays. One dies. The other lives. We do not know why and we can only trust God. There was the same love, the same prayer …

'Michael, Jimmy is in intensive care in the hospital with meningitis. Can you come and anoint him with oil?' I went at once.

The tiny baby boy was lying motionless in a cot – his life hanging in the balance. We prayed. I anointed him with oil. We entrusted him to the Lord. That night his recovery began. Some might say, 'Perhaps he would have recovered anyway', but we were very aware God was present in that hospital room as we prayed …

In our second curacy, the church was learning to trust God more in prayer. In this process, I asked my 'boss' if I could preach about healing on the next Sunday evening – I explained the line I would take. He agreed. On Tuesday, he was rushed into hospital, seriously ill. On the Wednesday, the church prayer gathering took place as usual but now was sparked into deeper trust and prayer. The Lord chose to stop the internal bleeding at the exact time we prayed. It seemed a specific encouragement to us in trusting prayer and, in the following weeks and months, the prayer gathering moved to another level. The answer was thus both for the patient *and* for the church! We would need to go on from there to trust Him even when there was no such dramatic answer …

The ministry of prayer for those in need should be a high priority for *all* Christians. As we have explained in this book, most people do not recover in the ways I have mentioned above, but some do, and even those who do not recover are blessed in various ways as we pray for them.

One of the much-valued privileges of being a Christian within the family of the church is that we support one another, and so can seek and rely on the prayer support of many in the family. Some churches organise prayer 'chains', where the needs and updates are passed from one to another. We might also find support if we belong to a small group, such as a study group or fellowship group, where the prayer should be focused so that we can feel wonderfully upheld.

One church may organise special evenings of prayer for those needing God's healing hand. Another church may have regular prayer gatherings, perhaps four times a year, to give special opportunity for such prayer and personal care. One way of doing this in a large meeting is by organising the chairs into a number of circles, so that the congregation can split into small groups of people enabling each person to share if they wish, but also giving the opportunity for personal, private prayer. At the same time, there should be provision for going to pray with a trained prayer supporter.

In James 5:13–16, we see how the Jerusalem church, under James' leadership, approached prayer for healing. We are given the example of when a member of the church is too sick to get to the fellowship meetings (which would be the normal setting for such prayer), so the leaders come to the bedside. There is prayer over the sick person and the anointing with oil. There is opportunity for confession of sin so as not to have a barrier between the sick person and God (because it is *very occasionally* the case that unconfessed sin or internal bitterness has caused or aggravated the sickness).

One sin that can deeply affect our health and block our healing is that of non-forgiveness. It has been so frustrating across the years to see people who say, 'I will never forgive', and who are consumed by non-forgiveness and bitterness. As the Lord's Prayer reminds us, forgiveness of others has to happen if we are to know the Lord's forgiveness for ourselves. When anyone refuses to forgive others who have hurt or wronged them, then the anger not only festers in their soul, but their health is affected severely. They become gnarled with bitterness. Patient ministry to bring such a person to forgive is not easy, but has immediate impact on health when it happens. In contrast, we have seen in recent years some remarkable forgiveness expressed by Christian parents towards the murderers of their son or daughter, and a peace bathing their spirit as a result. The world was appalled at the photo of a young child running naked and burnt, her face full of terror, after the dropping of a napalm bomb in the Vietnam War. Could she ever forgive? Her suffering was appalling. As an adult, Phai Thi Kim Phuc cried to God: 'If you are real, help me forgive.' He did. At a Vietnam rally, John Plummer, who was in charge of the flight that dropped the napalm bomb, asked her, 'Do you forgive me?' 'Yes, I do,' she replied, and cried and cried. Total release.

At first sight, James makes a bold promise: '... the prayer offered in faith will make the sick person well; the Lord will raise him up' (v.15) and 'so that you may be healed' (v.16). However, the word translated 'well' here is *sozo*, the main meaning of which is 'save' (which is the word used in the NRSV and NKJV). Furthermore, the word used for 'raise' can also mean 'to excite, awaken, rouse, raise the dead'. And the word used for 'heal' means 'to heal, cure, and restore from a state of sin and condemnation'. Thus, what is meant here could be straightforward healing, but it could also be about a wonderful encouragement to the spirits of the sick person to draw him or her back into fresh faith and peace, especially if in the latter stages of terminal illness.

It is also a loving responsibility of the Church to care and pray for those members who are away from the area, especially those in service for Christ. We see this in regard to healing in Philippians 2:27–30. Here is Paul's tender account of Epaphroditus, who had been such a great help to him. Paul writes that he 'was ill, and almost died' and '… almost died for the work of Christ'. It seems that it was a lengthy illness. The Philippians were distressed for him, and then Epaphroditus was distressed that they were distressed! We can empathise with this situation. However, 'God had mercy on him, and not on him only but also on me, to spare me sorrow upon sorrow'. This was clearly a relief to all and a cause for thankfulness, not least for Paul who so valued his help. We assume there was much prayer for Epaphroditus and his healing. There was also clearly much care, but there was no sudden healing. Most of us can align with this pilgrimage of love and looking to God as loved ones near or far have gone through serious illness. Indeed, Paul must have felt the pain when, as he writes in 2 Timothy 4:20, 'I left Trophimus sick in Miletus'. Timothy is told to take wine for his stomach's sake and because of his 'frequent illnesses' in 1 Timothy 5:23. There is no mention of healing for either of them.

Prayer for the sick and for healing is answered in several different ways:

- *We do see some clearly healed.*
- *In some, we see the disease stopped or slowed down.*
- *Help and fresh insight is given to the medical team as they treat the patient.*
- *Others will speak of the deep experience of being prayed for and*

of being upheld by God as their illness continues to progress.
- Some will find fresh faith and courage, becoming more effective witnesses to grace in their illness.
- Many will experience the love of God at a deepening level.
- Some will find new confidence in salvation through Christ, and new confidence about eternal life.

Our prayer for our sick brothers and sisters is offering them to God, bringing them to Him, surrounding them with our love as we stand with them before the Lord. We do not dictate how God should answer, for His ways are higher than our ways, and His thoughts higher than our thoughts (see Isa. 55:9), but we believe He will answer as He sees best within His overall purposes. We have brought the person to Him and will go on doing so, but our hearts can be at peace because we can do no greater thing for them in their need.

When praying for others in such challenges to their life, I often pray that they may know God's hug of love in a special way, for their deepest need is usually for *care* rather than *cure*.

Praying for healing is a matter of deep involvement with our heavenly Father. Some Christians are specially gifted in this ministry of healing (1 Cor. 12:9,28). It is godliness and prayerfulness that marks out true healing intercessors, and they have humility and honesty. John Wimber,[2] for example, inspired many regarding healing as confirming the Word but said, according to D.A. Carson,[3] that only 2 per cent were healed at his meetings. This humble honesty was also demonstrated by his being open about his courageous battling with throat cancer, from which he died. Nevertheless, Carson notes, there did not seem to be any balancing theology of suffering that could see triumphant faith when not healed.

An example of personal prayer for healing

In 2 Corinthians 12:7–11 we are given an example of how to pray when we have a physical need. We learn from Paul, a 'master-Christian', a man of deep closeness to God, a man of thought-through theology, a 'servant of Christ' and a man who had known more suffering in his life than most other people, as we see in the list in 2 Corinthians 11:23–33. He tells us in 2 Corinthians 12:7 about the 'thorn in the flesh' that is hampering his life and ministry: 'To keep me from becoming conceited because of these ... great revelations, there was given me a thorn in my flesh, a messenger of Satan, to torment me.'

The Greek word for flesh does indeed mean 'flesh' or 'body'. It is thus almost certainly a physical experience. Some want to explain the word as referring to our carnal nature, but this does not fit in with praying for it to be removed. Some think it is a specific opponent, but again this seems highly unlikely because it was an ongoing suffering and was to be met by prayer, whereas his opponents were met by robust argument and forceful teaching; so the vast majority of commentators agree that it has to be what it says ... in-the-flesh, physical suffering. A 'thorn' is actually a shaft of wood, a sharpened stake, and is something that is not self-inflicted. It is thus something Paul did not want and did not like!

Paul regards it as a messenger of Satan to 'torment' him. The word 'torment' is a possible clue to Paul's condition, as it literally means 'to hit with a fist, to strike with the knuckles, to buffet'. It is suggested that this is a good description of malarial fever that makes one feel helpless, or a migraine, but basically we do not know! How good that we don't, or else we would limit the text to that particular illness instead of applying its teaching to all illness.

Paul also shows in verse 7 of 2 Corinthians 12 that one of the major impacts of debilitating illness is to keep one from being too conceited about being a great Christian achiever, or someone with special spiritual experiences, or someone who is a 'success' in their Christian life or ministry. The NIV has this at the start of the verse, but actually it occurs twice in most versions of the Greek New Testament as the NRSV shows: 'Therefore, to keep me from becoming too elated, a thorn was given to me in the flesh, a messenger of Satan to torment me, to keep me from being too elated.' F.F. Bruce said that the thorn is to puncture our pride. Paul is in no doubt about its beneficial effect!

All illness is to be prayed about

Verse 8 of 2 Corinthians 12 ('Three times I pleaded with the Lord to take it away from me') indicates that illness is to be prayed about. This may seem obvious, but it really does need to be stated and acted upon, because there are those who do not think any healings happen by God's special intervention today. They do not pray because they do not expect an answer. Paul says he prayed the same prayer three times. Was that on three different days, or for three long periods of prayer, or even three times in one day? Was it three times in a month, a year, or longer? How good that we don't know, or else we would say, 'Until you have prayed for so long in the same way as Paul, you will not have God's response.' It is so sad that Christians can descend into a sort of legalism like that. It comes in other ways, such as saying that unless you anoint or unless you lay hands on the sick person, they will not be healed. I reply that although a patient may be encouraged by hands and oil, and they are symbols of serious prayer, it is *God* who heals.

When praying for healing, we should also remember all those who seek to help medically, all who are researching ways of finding cures and new ways of treating damage to the body externally or internally, and all who are seeking to find better ways of preventing illnesses. They are often going to be the means through which prayer is answered. When praying for others, prayer needs to be with deep empathy and not just some pronounced 'formula'. In remembering the sick person, we should also remember to pray that their nearest and dearest may have great grace and peace, especially when they are having to cope with distressing symptoms, the demands of exhausting nursing, and personal distress.

Overall, personal prayer for healing means coming to God in believing prayer for ourselves, our loved ones, our friends, our church family, for all known to us. We come believing God is able to heal, but not demanding that He must do so. He is not there to do our will, whereas we should want to do His will. Some people say that if we add 'if it be your will', this is a 'cop out' of faith. I point them first to 1 John 5:14, 'This is the confidence we have in approaching God: that if we ask anything *according to his will*, he hears us (italics mine)', and then to the passionate prayer of our Lord in Luke 22:42–44: 'Father, if you are willing, take this cup from me; yet not my will, but yours be done.' Here we see 'Your will be done' not as a barrier to faith prayer, but as the framework for it. Dare they accuse our Lord of having no faith? There was great intensity in His prayer, His sweat was as drops of blood and an angel came to strengthen Him, but He prayed, 'Your will, not Mine be done.' Also in Hebrews 5:7 we read: 'In the days of his flesh, Jesus offered up prayers and supplications, with loud cries and tears, to the one who was able to save him from death, *and he was heard because of his reverent submission*' (NRSV, italics mine). Our Lord was heard, but His passion and death still happened. Indeed, the writer to the Hebrews continues: 'Although he was a son, he learned obedience from what he suffered' (v.8). In the same way, we grow into the depths of God as we reach to Him from the heart, and learn to trust and obey Him in every experience of life: 'I cling to you; your right hand upholds me.'

NOTES

1   The baby referred to is now a fine Christian man. This was a particular encouragement to our church in its prayer life.

2   John Richard Wimber, 1939–97, charismatic pastor and one of the founding teachers of the Vineyard Movement.

3   D.A. Carson, *How Long, O Lord?* (Leicester: IVP, 1982) p.124.

SEVENTEEN

Sufficient grace; complete power

> But he said to me, 'My grace is sufficient for you, for my power is made perfect in weakness.' Therefore I will boast all the more gladly about my weaknesses, so that Christ's power may rest on me. That is why, for Christ's sake, I delight in weaknesses, in insults, in hardships, in persecutions, in difficulties. For when I am weak, then I am strong. (2 Corinthians 12:9–10)

'My grace is sufficient for you ...'

In this moving passage, we learn from the deeply prayerful apostle Paul how to handle life if God does not heal us or remove whatever 'thorn' is hurting us. Some would call this 'dealing with unanswered prayer', but I do not think any prayer is unanswered. God will meet us with special grace and power. Paul knew that deeply in his life and speaks from the heart of that experience when he begins 2 Corinthians by praising God as 'the Father of compassion and the God of all comfort' (1:3). The comfort he has known has reached deeply into his soul and permeated his whole being.

The words 'my grace is sufficient for you, for my power is made perfect in weakness', from 2 Corinthians 12:9, are very precious to those who have taken them to heart as they suffer. Numerous Christians have told me that it is their favourite and most valued text from the Bible. It is definitely one of mine!

But what does Paul mean by 'grace' here? Elsewhere, in Ephesians 1, 'grace' is in the greeting (v.2); we are to live as children of God 'to the praise of his glorious grace, which he has freely given us in the One he loves' (v.6), and the redemption we have received through his blood, the forgiveness of sins is 'in accordance with the riches of God's grace

... lavished on us' (vv.7–8). So grace is the unmerited free gift of God to us in redeeming us into His family. But now the word is used in 2 Corinthians 12:9 in the context of suffering. For many the word 'grace' is a vague word, which James Denney described as 'a vague benignity, which may fairly be spoken of as a "smile"'.[1]

However, in 2 Corinthians 12:9, the word is associated with 'strength' or 'power' which is 'made perfect in weakness'. This gives us the clue. Our salvation was from a state of helplessness; we could not save ourselves. Now his thorn in the flesh has weakened him, even at times leaving him unable to do anything when the illness hits, and this is when grace can most fully operate by giving strength other than one's own. So powerful is this grace that he even 'delights' in his weaknesses. He had proven in the experiences of suffering that God's grace was indeed sufficient: 'For when I am weak, then I am strong' (v.10).

So how did Paul come to understand that God was not going to heal him, but instead give sufficient grace and power to cope with his 'thorn'? The only explanation can be that Paul walked closely with his Lord. Philippians 3:10 ('I want to know Christ and the power of his resurrection and the fellowship of sharing in his sufferings') shows just how much he longed to know Christ more and more. It is only in such communion with God that we can be open to hear Him, and be open to see suffering as something to be expected, something which can be turned to glory as we identify with our crucified Lord.

Rick Warren,[2] internationally famous author of *The Purpose-Driven Life*, wrote in a magazine article about his wife, Kay, contracting cancer:

> 'we discovered quickly that, in spite of the prayers of hundreds and thousands of people, God is not going to heal Kay or make it easy for her, and yet God has strengthened her character, given her a ministry of helping other people, given her a testimony, drawn her closer to Him and to people.'

He does not tell us how this conviction came, but clearly God brought them in prayer to understand what He was saying to them.

God's assurance is about His power in 'weakness'. This presumably refers to the weakening impact of the 'thorn' in Paul's flesh. The word 'weakness' (or 'weak' or 'weaknesses') is used four times in two verses: 2 Corinthians 12:9–10. From the Greek word *asthenia*, it is used several times in the Gospels for illness; for example, the woman who is crippled in Luke 13:11, and the crowds gathering to be healed of their diseases in Luke 5:15. It is used in that memorable sentence about Lazarus: 'he whom you love is ill' (John 11:3, NRSV). It is clearly about *weakening* illness, and thus we can be 99 per cent certain that the 'thorn in the flesh' is a physical illness. However, it is also the word used in Matthew 8:17: 'He took our infirmities and carried our diseases.' Those who wish to persuade us that everyone can be healed because of this verse, arguing that the cross dealt with all our sins and all our diseases, and thus that all can be saved and all healed, should see that the same word is used in 2 Corinthians 12:9–10 where 'weakness' is something we should boast about, if that is how God's glory is to be shown in our lives. It will not be until we are in the new heaven and the new earth that we will actually be *free* of sin and *free* of illnesses. That will indeed be because of our Lord's gift of salvation through his dying for us on the cross.

Paul's acceptance that healing, the removal of the 'thorn', was not God's way for him on this occasion would have been pounced on by the self-appointed 'super-apostles' who had infiltrated the Corinthian church (2 Cor. 11:5). It was because of them that Paul wrote 2 Corinthians. The whole of this letter is about the theme of suffering. So passionate does Paul feel about what is happening that he does not pause for personal greetings at the start of the letter. It seems that these smooth-talking infiltrators (2 Cor. 11:6) took the line that if Christians were suffering there was something wrong with their faith. Because Paul had suffered so much in the cause of the gospel, they sought to persuade the Corinthians that he was not reliable, implying that his faith must be questionable. In 2 Corinthians 13:3 we read that the Corinthian church was demanding proof that Christ was speaking through Paul, which was an unbelievable thing to do considering it was Paul who came into the filthy, immoral city of Corinth with the gospel and, against all human odds, saw conversions as he preached

'Jesus Christ and him crucified'. Yes, he had trembled and his words were not humanly persuasive, but they were with 'the Spirit's power' (1 Cor. 2:2–5). Right from the start, he showed power in weakness; he was spiritually effective even when (or perhaps because) he was personally afraid.

The super-apostles (Paul calls them 'false apostles, deceitful workmen, masquerading as apostles of Christ' in 2 Corinthians 11:13) are equivalent to today's 'prosperity gospel' proponents. Typically from the more affluent parts of the world, these Christians manipulate the Scriptures to 'prove' that if we aren't successful, prosperous and trouble-free, we can't be bona fide believers. Neither the super-apostles nor the 'prosperity gospel' advocates would approve of Paul's remonstration in 2 Corinthians 11:7: 'Was it a sin for me to lower myself in order to elevate you by preaching the gospel of God to you *free of charge?*' (italics mine). Never-ending success and suffering-free Christianity is their message. It seems so much more attractive than the true gospel which Paul preached – is it any wonder so many are attracted to this 'heaven now' teaching? Paul said they were preaching another Christ, 'a different spirit' and 'a different gospel' (2 Cor. 11:4).

Hopefully, most Christians will stand with Paul in advocating a balance between praying for healing and being open to God's will if healing is not the way. Though we may see many touches from heaven on earth which will encourage us, we must accept that we are still pilgrims, en route for 'home'.

There are those who dismiss the balanced approach of 2 Corinthians 12:9 and are adamant that *everyone* can be healed and, if they are not, that they must have insufficient faith or hidden and unconfessed sin. However sincere those who teach this may be (seemingly deriving their ideas from the selective use of Scripture), they do not seem to realise the deep damage it causes to very many fellow Christians (and, indeed, non-believers). John Wimber did not teach this but instead, according to D.A. Carson, he was 'careful to insist that there is no New Testament warrant that any individual ought to be healed or else charged with inadequate faith'.[3]

I hear time and time again from pastors and lay people about the sad experiences of those who were told by a well-meaning believer that God heals *everyone* who prays in faith. Then, they tell me, when the sick person does not get healed, or even dies, the shattering of expectation often severely damages or destroys faith in God, and the damage takes years to repair (and sadly, it can sometimes be irreparable). I recall one couple where the husband was dying and had a marvellous faith. It was a privilege to visit him, and a few hours before he died I read part of 2 Corinthians 4 and 5 to him. The room seemed alight with the presence of God. It was holy ground. Yet his wife insisted right up to the moment he died that God must heal him. The result was her tragic loss of faith in God. It was so sad and so unnecessary, as 2 Corinthians 12:9 shows us.

When I was rector of All Souls, Langham Place, I received a letter from a house church in south London. It said that their pastor had contracted cancer and they had prayed earnestly that he would be healed. He wasn't. He died. So, the letter said: 'we prayed for his resurrection from the dead. He wasn't raised.' Then the writer added these chilling words: 'The whole church has lost its faith.'

These misconceptions about healing also affect care. One very sad sequence was when a godly pastor who contracted cancer at a young age so believed he must be healed that when I went to visit him, he said: 'No need to visit me, Michael, as I am going to be healed.' He would cry out to God in the night, and only in the last forty-eight hours of his earthly life did he let go and put himself into the arms of his beloved Saviour and Lord. The congregation was terribly sad at losing him, but also sad that the dear man had not been able to turn that terminal experience into a witness of grace and glory, as a senior lay person had wonderfully and powerfully done in similar circumstances the year before.

The most terrible travesty we hear about all too often is when people say to a seriously ill person, or to those close to them, 'If you had more faith, you (or they) would be healed' or, 'You must have unconfessed sin'. Even worse is when they say to a recently bereaved mother, 'Your baby would not have died if you had had more faith' or again,

'You must have had hidden sin'. They are acting like Job's so-called comforters. It is because they are convinced that the Scriptures clearly teach that everyone should be healed that they have to find a reason when there is no healing. My heart has bled for those who have been deeply hurt and wounded by such loveless statements and, as I know from years in ministry and as so many pastors and leaders tell me, a huge amount of loving care and counselling has been required to help restore the person who, already wounded by bereavement, has been further wounded by those judgmental remarks. If anyone reading this has been wounded in this way, I hope they will take hold of the truth of 2 Corinthians 12:9 and be rid of any lurking sense of guilt.

DAVID WATSON

David C.K. Watson[4] was one of God's most outstanding evangelists and ministers of the 1960s and 1970s. His ministry was greatly blessed and great crowds gathered to hear him. He had embraced the 'charismatic movement'. He and his church had prayed for four people with terminal cancer, and all four died. He then visited the Vineyard in the USA and saw the powerful preaching and healing ministry of John Wimber. Not long after, David was diagnosed with terminal cancer of the liver. He was given about a year to live. It brought literally tens of thousands to their knees in prayer for him. John Wimber and his team flew across from the USA, but David's cancer simply progressed and he died. His book *Fear No Evil*, written in those final months, is immensely moving and courageous; a great witness. We have sorely missed him and his ministry.

David was so evidently a wonderful example of a godly man, much beloved, walking close to his Lord, believing strongly in healing, seeking cleansing from every sin known and unknown, being prayed for by people all over the world, who was still not healed. Surely this would stop the unbalanced claims. Yet, not long afterwards, someone was heard saying, 'He must have had hidden sin'. How untrue! How appallingly unloving! How hurtful to his widow!

SAMUEL ZWELLER

Samuel Zweller is mentioned in Hallesby's great book *Prayer*, which truly is a classic.[5] Zweller lived in Switzerland and majored on the 'care of people who were mentally or physically ill, tired, or worn out nervously', even though he himself had a life-threatening illness. He had a remarkable gift of grace, of healing by prayer. Hallesby heard him praying with 'quietness and confidence', rather than with 'fervency and emotion', because 'he knew God well': 'He merely told God what was needed.' His prayers were 'reverent, but natural, conversations with God, as though God were sitting in the first pew and Zweller was standing before him'. Hallesby noticed that in the end his prayers were actually one prayer, namely, that the name of God might be glorified. He would pray for miracles, but always added 'if it will glorify your name'.

Miracle-working prayer was not to Zweller a means of escaping tribulation, but only a means of glorifying God. So he often added to his prayer these words: 'If it will glorify your name more, then let them remain sick; but, if that be your will, give them power to glorify your name through their illness.'

That really is the balance of 2 Corinthians 12:7–10. Zweller gives us the template for balanced, biblical, humble, believing prayer for healing.

... my power is made perfect in weakness

Once Paul has the understanding from his Lord that healing is not to be God's way, he picks up his life with fresh vigour and purpose. One young man once said to me, after hearing me talk about the 'my grace' text, 'I suppose Paul then put up with it'. But I told him to look at the passage! Paul sees it as a way of power, he *boasts* of his weaknesses (*asthenia*), he *delights* in weaknesses, insults, hardships, persecutions and difficulties! Why? Because he knows that, when he is weak, he is thrown more upon his Lord, which will mean power to live to Christ's glory. It is breathtaking stuff. I want to stand up and applaud. I am thrilled at such a witness. I then realise I must follow such an example in my own life. Lord, help me so to do.

To the super-apostles and 'prosperity gospel' proponents, this would be ridiculous and defeatist. They only want trouble-free and comfortable Christianity, with prosperity and health.

The key to Paul's response is the priority he gives in his life to forwarding the gospel of Christ and His kingdom. We recall how this is expressed in Philippians 1:12 onward. He is in chains in prison, but he sees that this has actually advanced the gospel; rivals preach Christ from wrong motives while he suffers, but still he is overjoyed that Christ is preached; facing possible death, he longs for courage to exalt Christ in his body, whether by life or death: 'For to me, to live is Christ and to die is gain' (v.21). When this is the priority of our life, suffering and healing are of secondary importance.

Paul would have liked the words on the jug of an old Friendly Society:

> **The loss of gold is much,**
> **the loss of health is more,**
> **but losing Christ is such a loss**
> **as no man can restore**

As one studies the Gospels and Acts, this same priority of the gospel is seen. The watershed of Matthew, Mark and Luke is the moment when Jesus asks the disciples who they think He is and Peter declares: 'You are the Christ, the Son of the living God' (Matt. 16:16). Up to that point there have been numerous healings recorded, with about thirteen references in each Gospel. Then, after the watershed, everything turns towards the cross. Mark records three occasions in the next two chapters when Jesus teaches the disciples that He is to suffer, die and rise again. There are only two or three references to healing in Matthew and Mark and about six in Luke after the watershed. This seems to be because their main purpose had been to show who Jesus was (John uses the term 'signs', eg in John 2:11 at Cana: 'He thus revealed his glory, and his disciples put their faith in him'), or it might be that healings continued but nothing was allowed to be more important than the cross and the means of salvation wrought there; we do not know. Certainly, in Acts there is a mix between healings opening up the hearing of the gospel, of affirming who Jesus is, and validating the authority of the apostles. Yet the whole thrust is the priority of the gospel.

It is this priority which causes Paul to respond so strongly in 2 Corinthians 12:9–10. If God is not going to take away his 'thorn', then he will turn it into a means of witness; he will not grumble or feel let down, but be renewed in his gospel mission. If this is how God is going to strengthen him and the impact of his ministry, he will delight in and boast of his weakness. It is to be a theatre of grace in his life. His whole attitude is transformed.

Before Paul finishes his second letter to the Corinthians, he brings a clinching blow about weakness and power. In 2 Corinthians 13:3–4 he points them to their suffering yet all-powerful Lord Jesus. '[Christ] is not weak in dealing with you, but is powerful among you. For to be sure, he was crucified in weakness, yet he lives by God's power. Likewise, we are weak in him, yet by God's power we will live with him to serve you.'

It is that Christ, our Saviour and Lord, to whom our eyes must turn as we come to the end of this book. He is our inspiration, our model, our helper and our guide.

He showed us how to live with suffering, as 'a man of sorrows', 'familiar with suffering', who was 'pierced for our transgressions', 'oppressed and afflicted' (see Isa. 53). He knew suffering to the depths.

As Stanley Jones wrote:

> **He told us not to escape suffering but to use it. Christ suggests that we are to take up pain, calamity, injustice and persecution, into the purpose of our lives and make them contribute to the higher ends – the ends for which we really live ... He does not explain suffering or explain it away – but he changes everything. He would turn the world's supreme tragedy into the world's supreme testimony – and He did![6]**

So, as Hebrews 12:1 puts it: 'let us throw off everything that hinders and the sin that so easily entangles, and let us run with perseverance the race marked out for us.' That race will, of course, vary enormously as to where we are in the world and what happens to us physically, but we are to 'fix our eyes on Jesus, the author and perfecter of our faith, who for the joy set before him *endured the cross, scorning its shame,* and sat down at the right hand of ... God' (v.2, italics mine).

We go in faith, our own great weakness feeling;
and needing more each day your grace to know;
yet from our hearts a song of triumph pealing,
'We trust in you, and in your name we go.'[7]

May the words of our Lord in 2 Corinthians 12:9 be written on our hearts, and lived out in our lives:

'My grace is sufficient for you, for my power is made perfect in weakness.'

NOTES

1   James Denney, *The Second Epistle to the Corinthians* (London: Hodder & Stoughton, 1894).

2   Dr Richard Duane ('Rick') Warren; founder and senior pastor of Saddleback mega-church in Lake Forest, California, and prolific author. From an interview conducted in February 2004 by Jim Daley, the executive editor for *Decision* magazine, a publication of the Billy Graham Evangelistic Association. My thanks to him for allowing me to quote him.

3   D.A. Carson, *How Long, O Lord?*, (Leicester: IVP, 1982), p.124.

4   See Chapter 10, note 3.

5   O. Hallesby, *Prayer* (Leicester: IVP, 1948), p.100.

6   E. Stanley Jones, *Christ and Human Suffering* (London: Hodder & Stoughton, 1933).

7   Edith Cherry (1872–97), 'We Trust in You Our Shield and Our Defender'; in this version, Jubilate Hymns.

Courses and seminars

Publishing and new media

Conference facilities

Transforming lives

CWR's vision is to enable people to experience personal transformation through applying God's Word to their lives and relationships.

Our Bible-based training and resources help people around the world to:
- Grow in their walk with God
- Understand and apply Scripture to their lives
- Resource themselves and their church
- Develop pastoral care and counselling skills
- Train for leadership
- Strengthen relationships, marriage and family life and much more.

Our insightful writers provide daily Bible-reading notes and other resources for all ages, and our experienced course designers and presenters have gained an international reputation for excellence and effectiveness.

CWR's Training and Conference Centre in Surrey, England, provides excellent facilities in an idyllic setting – ideal for both learning and spiritual refreshment.

CWR Applying God's Word
to everyday life and relationships

CWR, Waverley Abbey House,
Waverley Lane, Farnham,
Surrey GU9 8EP, UK

Telephone: +44 (0)1252 784700
Email: info@cwr.org.uk
Website: www.cwr.org.uk

Registered Charity No 294387
Company Registration No 1990308

Draw strength and hope from the Son of God

The God we see in Jesus did not study our sufferings from a distance in a cold and detached way. His ability to heal our wounds flows from the fact that He Himself *experienced* our wounds. This insightful DVD resource will increase your awareness that Jesus is committed to us and can relieve and support us through the pain we experience in life, giving us hope and strength to face whatever comes our way.

Presented by CWR's Chief Executive Mick Brooks at Wintershall Estate in Surrey with footage from their famous Life of Christ open-air production. Great for individual or small-group use – and ideal for Lent!

- **One DVD with five approx 15-minute sessions**
- **One personal study booklet with discussion starters, prayers and five weeks of daily Bible-reading notes. (One recommended for each group participant.)**

Jesus – The Wounded Healer DVD
Presented by Mick Brooks | Based on writings of Selwyn Hughes
EAN: 5027957001350